Francis Quarles, Christopher Harvey

The School of the Heart

or, The heart brought back again to Him, and instructed by Him: in forty-seven emblems

Francis Quarles, Christopher Harvey

The School of the Heart
or, The heart brought back again to Him, and instructed by Him: in forty-seven emblems

ISBN/EAN: 9783348030182

Printed in Europe, USA, Canada, Australia, Japan

Cover: Foto ©Lupo / pixelio.de

More available books at **www.hansebooks.com**

THE SCHOOL

OF

THE HEART.

Peruse this little Book; and thou wilt see
What thy Heart is, and what it ought to be.

THE SCHOOL

OF

THE HEART:

OR,

THE HEART

(OF ITSELF GONE AWAY FROM GOD)

BROUGHT BACK AGAIN TO HIM,
AND INSTRUCTED BY HIM.

IN FORTY-SEVEN EMBLEMS.

BY THE AUTHOR OF THE SYNAGOGUE,
ANNEXED TO HERBERT'S POEMS.

WHEREUNTO IS ADDED,

THE LEARNING OF THE HEART,
BY THE SAME HAND.

LONDON:
Printed for ALEX^r. HOGG, N° 16, Pater-Noster-Row.
MDCCLXXVIII.

THE

PREFACE.

IT is generally agreed, by the learned and the ferious, that *self-knowledge* is the *great knowledge:* and that an adept in univerfal fcience, if he remain a ftranger to himfelf, is only a lump of pride and conceit, and unfit for, not to fay an offence to, the fociety of his fellow-men.

SELF-KNOWLEDGE is the knowledge of what a man *really is*, confider'd in every relation in which he ftands, as a *moral agent*, as well as an *erect creature*. And it is to be prefumed, that this was the meaning of that renowned precept of the Pythian Apollo, "Nofce teipfum," *Know thyfelf.* Though it is impoffible for a man to know himfelf, without being acquainted with a fubject which is full of mortification to human pride and vanity.

WE hear much talk, in modern times, though there never was, perhaps, lefs reafon to talk, of *the dignity of human nature.* Human nature, in its original ftate, no doubt, was crowned with dignity and glory too. But alas! how is it now fallen! how is the gold become dim! how is the moft fine gold changed! For, fince the fall of man, there has been no true dignity in human nature, but as it was beheld in HIM, in whom was feen " the glory as of the only begotten of the Father, full of *grace* and *truth*."

THE ftate of the mind, or HEART, may be faid to determine the ftate and character of man. As *it* is, fo is *He*. And the facred writings every-where reprefent the heart as the feat of true religion, moral excellence, or virtue; which are in truth one and the fame: for there can be no virtue, where there is not true religion. But fuch is the wretched ftate of

every

every heart by nature, that is, while deſtitute of divine and ſpecial grace, that, as no contemptible writer obſerves,

" Heav'n's Sov'reign ſaves all beings but himſelf—
" That *hideous* ſight, a *naked human heart.*"

THE pride and ignorance of mankind may lead them to *reaſon* againſt this humbling, and, what they are pleaſe to term, gloomy repreſentation of things. But how abſurd to reaſon againſt ſtubborn fact! We appeal to *that*, and to *experience*. We appeal to *reaſon*, as well as to *revelation:* and both, we are perſuaded, will tell us, that thoſe, who prate about the dignity of human nature and its moral excellence, until it be renewed after the image of God, which ſin has obliterated, are only indulging the pleaſures of *imagination*, and need much inſtruction in ——
THE SCHOOL OF THE HEART.

THE following pages bear this title: and as they are deſigned to preſent us with the anatomy of the human heart in a moral or ſpiritual view, to expoſe its diſorders, their nature, and their cure; it is hoped they may prove of no little ſervice to the beſt in-

[... in ...]?
For, as well
ely to p
diseas'd,

THE CONTENTS

TO EACH

ODE.

THE Infection of the Heart,	Page 8
The Taking away of the Heart,	11
The Darkness of the Heart,	14
The Absence of the Heart,	17
The Vanity of the Heart,	20
The Oppression of the Heart,	23
The Covetousness of the Heart,	26
The Hardness of the Heart,	29
The Division of the Heart,	32
The Infatiableness of the Heart,	35
The Returning of the Heart,	38
The Pouring out of the Heart,	41
The Circumcision of the Heart,	44
The Contrition of the Heart,	47
The Humiliation of the Heart	50
The Softening of the Heart,	53
The Cleansing of the Heart,	56
The Grieving of the Heart,	59
The Sacrifice of the Heart,	62
The Weighing of the Heart,	65
The Trying of the Heart,	68
The Sounding of the Heart,	71
The Levelling of the Heart,	74

THE CONTENTS.

The Renewing of the Heart,	Page 77
The Enlightening of the Heart,	80
The Table of the Heart,	83
The Tilling of the Heart,	86
The Seeding of the Heart,	89
The Watering of the Heart,	92
The Flowers of the Heart,	95
The Keeping of the Heart,	98
The Watching of the Heart,	101
The Wounding of the Heart,	104
The Inhabiting of the Heart,	107
The Enlarging of the Heart,	110
The Inflaming of the Heart,	113
The Ladder of the Heart,	116
The Flying of the Heart,	119
The Union of the Heart,	122
The Rest of the Heart,	125
The Bathing of the Heart,	128
The Binding of the Heart,	131
The Prop of the Heart,	134
The Scourging of the Heart,	137
The Hedging of the Heart,	140
The Fastening of the Heart,	143
The New Wine of the Heart,	149
The Learning of the Heart,	146
The Grammar of the Heart,	152
The Rhetoric of the Heart,	155
The Logic of the Heart,	158

THE SCHOOL OF THE HEART.

INTRODUCTION.

TURN in, my mind, wander not abroad:
Here's work enough at home; lay by that load
Of scatter'd thought, that clogs and cumbers thee:
Resume thy long-neglected liberty
Of self-examination: bend thine eye
Inward; confider where thy HEART doth lie,
How 'tis affected, how 'tis bufy'd: look,
What thou haft writ thyfelf in thine own book,
Thy confcience: here fet thou thyfelf to fchool;
Self-knowledge, 'twixt a wife man and a fool,
Doth make the difference; he that neglects
This learning, fideth with his own defects.
Doft thou draw back? Hath cuftom charm'd thee fo,
That thou canft relifh nothing but thy woe?
Find'ft thou fuch fweetnefs in thefe fugar'd lyes?
Have foreign objects fo ingrofs'd thine eyes?
Canft thou not hold them off? Haft thou an ear
To liften, but to what thou fhouldft not hear?
Art thou incapable of every thing,
But what thy fenfes to thy fancy bring?
Remember that thy birth and conftitution
Both promife better than fuch bafe confufion.
Thy birth's divine, from heav'n; thy compofure
Is fpirit, and immortal: thine inclofure

In

In walls of flesh; not to make thee debtor
For house-room to them, but to make them better:
Thy body's thy freehold, live then as lord,
Not tenant to thy own: some time afford
To view what state 'tis in: survey each part,
And, above all, take notice of thine HEART.
Such as that is, the rest is, or will be,
Better or worse, blame-worthy, or fault-free.
What! are the ruins such, thou art afraid,
Or else ashame'd, to see how 'tis decay'd?
Is't therefore thou art loth to see it such
As now it is, because it is so much;
Degenerated now from what it was,
And should have been? Thine ignorance, alas!
Will make it nothing better; and the longer
Evils are suffer'd grow, they grow the stronger:
Or hath thine understanding lost its light?
Hath the dark night of error dimm'd thy sight,
So that thou canst not, tho' thou wouldst, observe
All things amiss within thee, how they swerve
From the strait rules of righteousness and reason?
If so, omit not then this precious season:
'Tis yet school-time; as yet the door's not shut.
Hark how the Master calls. Come, let us put
Up our requests to him, whose will alone
Limits his pow'r of teaching, from whom none
Returns unlearned, that hath once a will
To be his scholar, and implore his skill.
Great Searcher of the heart, whose boundless sight
Discovers secrets, and doth bring to light
The hidden things of darkness, who alone
Perfectly know'st all things that can be known;
Thou know'st I do not, cannot, have no mind
To know mine heart: I am not only blind,

But

But lame, and liftlefs: thou alone canft make
Me able, willing: and the pains I take,
As well as the fuccefs, muft come from thee,
Who workeft both to will and do in me:
Having made me now willing to be taught,
Make me as willing to learn what I ought.
Or, if thou wilt allow thy fcholar leave
To choofe his leffon, left I fhould deceive
Myfelf again, as I have done too often,
Teach me to know my heart. Thou, thou canft foften,
Lighten, enliven, purify, reftore,
And make more fruitful than it was before,
Its hardnefs, darknefs, death, uncleannefs, lofs,
And barrennefs: refine it from the drofs,
And draw out all the dregs, heal ev'ry fore,
Teach it to know itfelf, and love thee more.
    Lord, if thou wilt, thou canft impart this fkill:
And as for other learning, take't who will.

The INFECTION of the Heart.

Acts v. 3.
Why hath Satan filled thine heart?

EPIG. I.

WHILST thou incline'ſt thy voice-inveigled ear,
  The ſubtil ſerpent's ſyren-ſongs to hear,
Thy heart drinks deadly poiſon drawn from hell,
And with a vip'rous brood of ſin doth ſwell.

ODE I.

The Soul.   1.
Profit and pleaſure, comfort, and content,
Wiſdom, and honor; and, when theſe are ſpent,
A freſh ſupply of more! Oh heav'nly words!
Are theſe the dainty fruits that this fair tree affords?

The Serpent.   2.
Yes, theſe and many more, if more may be,
All that the world contains, in this one tree
Contracted is. Take but a taſte, and try;
Thou may'ſt believe thyſelf, experience cannot lye.

The Soul.   3.
But thou may'ſt lye: and, with a falſe pretence
Of friendſhip, rob me of that excellence
Which my Creator's bounty hath beſtow'd,
And freely given me, to whom he nothing ow'd.

The Serpent.   4.
Strange compoſition! ſo credulous,
And at the ſame time ſo ſuſpicious!
This is the tree of knowledge; and until   [or ill?
Thou eat thereof, how canſt thou know what's good

CONTAGIO CORDIS.

Corde bibis stigium morbi mortisque venenum.
Hic te dum blandis decipit illecebris.

The INFECTION of the HEART.

While Satan thus deceives with flattring Breath,
Thy Heart drinks Poison in, Disease, and Death.

THE SCHOOL OF THE HEART.

The Soul.   5.
God infinitely good my Maker is,
Who neither will nor can do aught amiss.
The being I receiv'd, was that he sent,
And therefore I am sure must needs be excellent.

The Serpent.   6.
Suppose it be: yet doubtless he that gave
Thee such a being must himself needs have
A better far, more excellent by much:
Or else be sure that he could not have made thee such.

The Soul.   7.
Such as he made me, I am well content
Still to continue: for, if he had meant
I should enjoy a better state, he could
As easily have giv'n it, if he would.

The Serpent.   8.
And is it not all one, if he have giv'n
The means to get it? Must he still be driv'n
To new works of creation for thy sake?
Wilt thou not what he sets before thee deign to take?

The Soul.   9.
Yes, of the fruits of all the other trees
I freely take and eat: they are the fees
Allow'd me for the dressing, by the Maker:
But of this fatal fruit I must not be partaker.

The Serpent.   10.
And why? What danger can it be to eat
That which is good, being ordain'd for meat?
What wilt thou say? God made it not for food?

The Soul. 11.
Yes, good it is, no doubt, and good for meat:
But I am not allow'd thereof to eat.
My Maker's prohibition, under pain
Of death, the day I eat thereof, makes me refrain.

The Serpent. 12.
Faint-hearted fondling! canst thou fear to die,
Being a spirit and immortal? Fie.
God knows this fruit once eaten will refine
Thy grosser parts alone, and make thee all divine.

The Soul. 13.
There's something in it, sure: were it not good,
It had not in the midst of th' garden stood:
And being good, I can no more refrain
From wishing, than I can the fire to burn restrain.

14.
Why do I trifle then? What I desire
Why do I not? Nothing can quench the fire
Of longing, but fruition. Come what will,
Eat it I must, that I may know what's good and ill.

The Serpent. 15.
So, thou art taken now: that resolution
Gives an eternal date to thy confusion.
The knowledge thou hast got of good, and ill,
Is of good gone, and past; of evil, present still.

ABLATIO CORDIS.

*Scorta placent, et Vina placent, sic stultus inersque
Exanimisque Animus; sic sine Corde Cor est.*

The TAKING AWAY of the HEART.

*While Lust and Wine their beastly Joys impart,
The Mind grows dead; The Hearts without a Heart.*

THE SCHOOL OF THE HEART.

The TAKING AWAY of the Heart.

Hof. iv. 11.

Whoredom and wine, and new wine, take away the heart.

EPIG. 2.

*BASE luft and luxury, the fcum and drofs
Of hell-born pleafures, pleafe thee, to the lefs
Of thy foul's precious eye-fight, reafon; fo
Mindlefs thy mind, heartlefs thine heart doth grow.*

ODE II.

1.

Laid down already? and fo faft afleep?
 Thy precious heart left loofely on thine hand,
Which with all diligence thou fhouldeft keep,
 And guard againft thofe enemies, that ftand
Ready prepare'd to plunge it in the deep
 Of all diftrefs? Roufe thee, and underftand
  In time, what in the end thou muft confefs,
  That mifery at laft and wretchednefs
Is all the fruit that fprings from flothful idlenefs.

2.

Whilft thou lie'ft foaking in fecurity,
 Thou drown'ft thyfelf in fenfual delight,
And wallow'ft in debauched luxury,
 Which, when thou art awake and feeft, will fright
Thine heart with horror. When thou fhalt defcry,
 By the day-light, the danger of the night,
  Then, then, if not too late, thou wilt confefs,
  That endlefs mifery and wretchednefs
Is all the fruit that fprings from riotous excefs.

3.

Whilſt thou doſt pamper thy proud fleſh, and thruſt
  Into thy paunch the prime of all thy ſtore,
Thou doſt but gather fuel for that luſt,
  Which, boiling in thy liver, runneth o'er,
And frieth in thy throbbing veins, which muſt
  Needs vent, or burſt, when they can hold no more.
    But Oh conſider what thou ſhalt confeſs
    At laſt, that miſery and wretchedneſs
Is all the fruit that ſprings from luſtful wantonneſs.

4.

Whilſt thou doſt feed effeminate deſires
  With ſpumy pleaſures, whilſt fruition
The coals of luſt fans into flaming fires,
  And ſpurious delights thou doateſt on,
Thy mind through cold remiſſneſs ev'n expires,
  And all the active vigour of 't is gone.
    Take heed in time, or elſe thou ſhalt confeſs
    At laſt that miſery and wretchedneſs
Is all the fruit that ſprings from careleſſmindedneſs.

5.

Whilſt thy regardleſs ſenſe-diſſolved mind
  Lies by unbent, that ſhould have been thy ſpring
Of motion, all thy headſtrong paſſions find
  Themſelves let looſe, and follow their own ſwing;
Forgetful of the great account behind,
  As though there never would be ſuch a thing,
    But, when it comes indeed, thou wilt confeſs
    That miſery alone and wretchedneſs
Is all the fruit that ſprings from ſoul-forgetfulneſs.

Whilſt thou remember'ſt not thy latter end,
   Nor what a reck'ning thou one day muſt make,
Putting no difference 'twixt foe and friend,
   Thou ſuffer'ſt helliſh fiends thine heart to take,
Who, all the while thou trifleſt, do attend,
   Ready to bring it to the lake
      Of fire and brimſtone: where thou ſhalt confeſs,
      That endleſs miſery and wretchedneſs
Is all the fruit that ſprings from ſtupid heartleſſneſs.

The Darkness of the Heart.

Rom. i. 21.

Their foolish heart was darkened.

EPIG. 3.

SUCH *cloudy shadows have eclips'd thine heart,*
As nature cannot parallel, nor art:
Unless thou take my light of truth to guide thee,
Blackness of darkness will at length betide thee.

ODE III.

1.

Tarry, O tarry, lest thine heedless haste
Hurry thee headlong unto hell at last:
 See, see, thine heart's already half-way there;
 Those gloomy shadows, that encompass it,
 Are the vast confines of th' infernal pit.
  O stay; and if thou lov'st not light, yet fear
   That fatal darkness, where
   Such danger doth appear.

2.

A night of ignorance hath overspread
Thy mind and understanding: thou art led
 Blindfolded by unbridled passion:
 Thou wand'rest in the crooked ways of error,
 Leading directly to the king of terror:
  The course thou takest, if thou holdest on,
   Will bury thee anon
   In deep destruction.

Emb. 3.

CORDIS TENEBRÆ.

*Heu tenebras Cordis! Tenebræ quibus exteriores
Succedent, ni sit Lux tibi luce mea.*

The DARKNESS of the HEART.

*O the Heart's Darkness! which without my Light,
Would lead to deeper Glooms, and endless Night.*

3.

Whilft thou art thus deprived of thy fight,
Thou know'ft no diff'rence between noon and night,
   Tho' the fun fhine, yet thou regard'ft it not.
My love-alluring beauty cannot draw thee,
Nor doth my mind-amazing terror awe thee:
   Like one that had both good and ill forgot,
      Thou careft not a jot
     What falleth to thy lot.

4.

Thou art become unto thyfelf a ftranger,
Obferveft not thine own defert, or danger,
   Thou know'ft not what thou doft, nor canft thou tell
Whither thou goeft: fhooting in the dark,
How canft thou ever hope to hit the mark?
   What expectation haft thou to do well,
      That art content to dwell
     Within the verge of hell?

5.

Alas, thou haft not fo much knowledge left,
As to confider that thou art bereft
   Of thine own eye-fight. But thou run'ft, as tho'
Thou faweft all before thee: whilft thy mind
To neareft neceffary things is blind.
   Thou knoweft nothing as thou ought'ft to know,
      Whilft thou efteemeft fo
     The things that are below.

6.

Would ever any, that had eyes, miftake
As thou art wont to do; no diff'rence make

                   Betwixt

Betwixt the way to heaven and to hell?
But, desperately devoted to destruction,
Rebel against the light, abhor instruction?
    As tho' thou didst desire with death to dwell,
        Thou hatest to hear tell
        How yet thou may'st do well.

7.

Oh that thou didst but see how blind thou art,
And feel the dismal darkness of thine heart!
    Then wouldst thou labour for, and I would lend,
My light to guide thee: that's not light alone,
But life, eyes, sight, grace, glory, all in one.
    Then shouldst thou know whither those by-ways bend,
        And that death in the end
        On darkness doth attend.

CORDIS FUGA.

Quam fugeret, Fugitiva, tuum Cor! si Cor haberes,
Non meminisse Mei, non Meminisse Sui.

The FLIGHT of the HEART.

Where's thy Heart flown? if thou a Heart hast got,
Who both Thyself and Me remembr'est not.

THE SCHOOL OF THE HEART. 17

The ABSENCE of the Heart.

Prov. xvii. 16.

Wherefore is there a price in the hand of a fool to get wisdom, seeing he hath no heart to it?

EPIG. 4.

*HADST thou an heart, thou fickle fugitive,
How would thine heart hate and disdain to live
Mindful of such vain trifles as these be!*

ODE IV.

The Soul. 1.
Brave, dainty, curious, rare, rich, precious things!
Able to make fate-blasted mortals blest,
Peculiar treasures, and delights for kings,
That having pow'r of all, would chuse the best.
  How do I hug mine happiness, that have
  Present possession of what others crave!

Christ. 2.
Poor, silly, simple, sense-besotted soul,
Why dost thou hug thy self-procured woes?
Release thy free-born thoughts, at least controul
Those passions that enslave thee to thy foes.
  How wouldst thou hate thyself, if thou didst know
  The baseness of those things thou prizest so!

The Soul. 3.
They talk of goodness, virtue, piety,
Religion, honesty, I know not what;
So let them talk for me: so long as I
Have goods and lands, and gold and jewels, that
  Both

Both equal and excel all other treasure, [sure ?
Why should I strive to make their pain my plea-

Christ. 4.
So swine neglect the pearls that lie before them,
Trample them under foot, and feed on draff * :
So fools gild rotten idols, and adore them,
Cast all the corn away, and keep the chaff.
    That ever reason should be blinded so,
    To grasp the shadow, let the substance go!

The Soul. 5.
All's but opinion that the world accounts
Matter of worth : as this or that man sets
A value on it, so the price amounts :
The sound of strings is vary'd by the frets,
    My mind's my kingdom : why should I withstand,
    Or question that, which I myself command ?

Christ. 6.
Thy tyrant passions captivate thy reason :
Thy lusts usurp the guidance of the mind :
Thy sense-led fancy barters good for geason † :
Thy seed is vanity, thine harvest wind :
    Thy rules are crooked, and thou writ'st awry :
    Thy ways are wand'ring, and thy mind to die.

The Soul. 7.
This table sums me myriads of pleasure :
That book enrolls mine honour's inventory :
These bags are stuff'd with millions of treasure :
Those writings evidence my state of glory :
    These bells ring heav'nly music in mine ears,
    To drown the noise of cumb'rous cares and fears.

---

* *Draff,* i. e. swill, or hogs-meat.   † *Geazon,* or *gazon,* i. e. a sod of earth.

Chrift.   8.
Thofe pleafures one day will procure thy pain:
That which thou glori'ft in, will be thy fhame:
Thou'lt find thy lofs in what thou thought'ft thy gain;
Thine honour will put on another name.
   That mufic, in the clofe, will ring thy knell;
   Inftead of heaven, toll thee into hell.

9.
But why do I thus wafte my words in vain
On one that's wholly taken up with toys;
That will not lofe one dram of earth, to gain
A full eternal weight of heav'nly joys?
   All's to no purpofe: 'tis as good forbear,
   As fpeak to one that hath no heart to hear.

The

The VANITY of the Heart.

Job xv. 31.

Let not him that is deceived truſt in vanity, for vanity ſhall be his recompence.

EPIG. 5.

*AMbition bellows with the wind of honour,
Puffs up the ſwelling heart that dotes upon her:
Which, fill'd with empty vanity, breathes forth
Nothing; but ſuch things as are nothing worth.*

ODE V.

1.

The bane of kingdoms, world's diſquieter,
Hell's heir apparent, Satan's eldeſt ſon,
Abſtract of ills, refined elixir,
And quinteſſence of ſin, ambition,
Sprung from th' infernal ſhades, inhabits here,
Making man's heart its horrid manſion,
   Which, tho' it were of vaſt extent before,
   Is now puft up, and ſwells ſtill more and more.

2.

Whole armies of vain thoughts it entertains,
Is ſtuff'd with dreams of kingdoms, and of crowns,
Preſumes of profit without care or pains,
Threatens to baffle all its foes with frowns,
In ev'ry bargain makes account of gains,
Fanſies ſuch frolick mirth as choaks and drowns
   The voice of conſcience, whoſe loud alarms
   Cannot be heard for pleaſure's counter-charms.

CORDIS VANITAS.

Ambitio Follis, vento distendit Honorum
Cor vanum: hinc spirat nil nisi grande Nihil.

The VANITY of the HEART.

Blown up with Honour's Wind, the Heart grows vain;
Tho' a great Nothing is the whole you gain.

THE SCHOOL OF THE HEART.

3.
Wer't not for anger, and for pity, who
Could chufe but fmile to fee vain-glorious men
Racking their wits, ftraining their finews fo,
That, thorough their tranfparent thinnefs, when
They meet with wind and fun, they quickly grow
Riv'led and dry, fhrink till they crack again,
   And all but to feem greater than they are? [bare:
Stretching their ftrength, they lay their weaknefs

4.
See how hell's fueller his bellows plies,
Blowing the fire that burnt too faft before :
See how the furnace flames, the fparkles rife
And fpread themfelves abroad ftill more and more!
See how the doting foul hath fix'd her eyes
On her dear fooleries, and doth adore,
   With hands and heart lift up, thofe trifling toys
Wherewith the devil cheats her of her joys!

5.
Alas, thou art deceiv'd; that glitt'ring crown,
On which thou gazeft, is not gold but grief,
That fceptre forrow: if thou take them down,
And try them, thou fhalt find what poor relief
They could afford thee, tho' they were thine own.
Didft thou command ev'n all the world in chief,
   Thy comforts would abate, thy cares increafe,
   And thy perplexed thoughts difturb thy peace.

6.
Thofe pearls fo thorough pierce'd, and ftrung together,
Tho' jewels in thine ears they may appear,
Will prove continu'd perils, when the weather
Is clouded once, which yet is fair and clear.

What will that fan, tho' of the fineſt feather,
Stead thee, the brunt of winds and ſtorms to bear?
  Thy flagging colours hang their drooping head,
  And the ſhrill trumpet's ſound ſhall ſtrike thee dead.

7.

Were all thoſe balls, which thou in ſport doſt toſs,
Whole worlds, and in thy power to command,
The gain would never countervail the loſs,
Thoſe ſlipp'ry globes will glide out of thine hand;
Thou canſt have no faſt hold but of the croſs,
And thou wilt fall, where thou doſt think to ſtand.
  Forſake theſe follies, then, if thou wilt live:
  Timely repentance may thy death reprive.

CORDIS AGGRAVATIO.

Crapula et Ebrietas, solidi duo pondera plumbi,
Nata Polo, sursum tendere Corda retant.

The OPPRESSION of the HEART.

With Gluttony, and Drunkenness possest,
By heaviest Weights the Heav'n-born Heart's opprest.

The OPPRESSION of the Heart.

Luke xxi. 34.
Take heed, left at any time your hearts be overcharged with surfeiting and drunkennefs.

EPIG. 6.

TWO maffy weights, furfeiting, drunkennefs,
  Like mighty logs of lead, do fo opprefs
The heav'n-born hearts of men, that to afpire
Upwards, they have nor power nor defire.

ODE VI.

1.
Monfter of fins ! See how th' inchanted foul,
  O'ercharge'd already, calls for more.
See how the hellifh fkinker * plies his bowl,
  And 's ready furnifhed with ftore,
    Whilft cups on every fide
    Planted, attend the tide.

2.
See how the piled difhes mounted ftand,
  Like hills advanced upon hills,
And the abundance both of fea and land
  Doth not fuffice, ev'n what it fills,
    Man's dropfy appetite,
    And cormorant delight.

* *Skinker;* i. e. butler.

3.

See how the poison'd body's puff'd and swell'd,
   The face inflamed glows with heat,
The limbs unable are themselves to wield,
   The pulses (death's alarm) do beat:
     Yet man sits still, and laughs,
     Whilst his own bane he quaffs.

4.

But where's thine heart the while, thou senseless sot?
   Look how it lieth crush'd, and quell'd,
Flat beaten to the board, that it cannot
   Move from the place where it is held,
     Nor upward once aspire
     With heavenly desire.

5.

Thy belly is thy god, thy shame thy glory,
   Thou mindest only earthly things;
And all thy pleasure is but transitory,
   Which grief at last and sorrow brings:
     The courses thou dost take
     Will make thine heart to ake.

6.

Is't not enough to spend thy precious time
   In empty idle compliment,
Unless thou strain (to aggravate thy crime)
   Nature beyond its own extent,
     And force it to devour
     An age within an hour?

7.
That which thou fwallow'ft is not loft alone,
 But quickly will revenged be,
By feizing on thine heart, which, like a ftone,
 Lies bury'd in the midft of thee,
  Both void of common fenfe
  And reafon's excellence.

8.
Thy body is difeafes' rendezvous,
 Thy mind the market-place of vice,
The devil in thy will keeps open houfe:
 Thou liv'ft, as though thou would'ft intice
  Hell-torments unto thee,
  And thine own devil be.

9.
Oh what a dirty dunghill art thou grown,
 A nafty ftinking kennel foul!
When thou awake'ft and feeft what thou haft done,
 Sorrow will fwallow up thy foul,
  To think how thou art foil'd,
  And all thy glory fpoil'd.

10.
Or if thou canft not be afhame'd, at leaft
 Have fome compaffion on thyfelf:
Before thou art transformed all to beaft,
 At laft ftrike fail, avoid the fhelf
  Which in that gulf doth lie,
  Where all that enter die.

The COVETOUSNESS of the Heart.

Mat. vi. 21.
Where your treasure is, there will your heart be also.

EPIG. 7.

DOST thou inquire, thou heartless wanderer,
Where thine heart is? Behold, thine heart is here.
Here thine heart is, where that is, which above
Thine own dear heart thou dost esteem and love.

ODE VII.

1.
See the deceitfulness of sin,
And how the devil cheateth worldly men:
They heap up riches to themselves, and then
   They think they cannot chuse but win,
      Though, for their parts,
      They stake their hearts.

2.
The merchant sends his heart to sea,
And there, together with his ship, 'tis tost:
If this by chance miscarry, that is lost,
   His confidence is cast away:
      He hangs the head,
      As he were dead.

CORDIS AVARITIA.

Cor ubi sit quæris Vaga et Excors ? scilicet hic est.
Est ubi, quod proprio plus tibi Corde placet.

The COVETOUSNESS of the HEART.

Here, Wandrer, may'st thou find thy Heart at last;
Where what is dearer than thy Heart is plac'd.

THE SCHOOL OF THE HEART. 27

3.
The pedlar cries, What do you lack ?
What will you buy ? and boasts his wares the best:
But offers you the refuse of the rest,
 As tho' his heart lay in his pack,
  Which greater gain
  Alone can drain.

4.
The ploughman furrows up his land,
And sows his heart together with his seed,
Which, both alike earth-born, on earth do feed,
 And prosper, or are at a stand:
  He and his field
  - Like fruit do yield.

5.
The broker and the scriv'ner have
The us'rer's heart in keeping with his bands * :
His soul's dear sustenance lies in their hands,
 And if they break, their shop's his grave,
  His int'rest is
  His only bliss.

6.
The money-hoarder in his bags
Binds up his heart, and locks it in his chest;
The same key serves to that, and to his breast,
 Which of no other heaven brags:
  Nor can conceit
  A joy so great.

* *Bands* ; i. e. bonds of obligation.

7.
So for the greedy landmonger:
The purchases he makes in ev'ry part
Take livery and seisin of his heart:
    Yet his insatiate hunger,
      For all his store,
    Gapes after more.

8.
Poor wretched muckworms, wipe your eyes,
Uncase those trifles that besot you so:
Your rich-appearing wealth is real woe,
    Your death in your desires lies.
      Your hearts are where
    You love and fear.

9.
Oh think not then the world deserves
Either to be belov'd or fear'd by you:
Give heaven these affections as its due,
    Which always what it hath preserves
      In perfect bliss
    That endless is.

APERTIO CORDIS LANCEA LONGINI.

Cor pia transadigat divini vulnere Amoris
Lancea, quae Jesu tincta cruore rubet.

The OPENING of the HEART with the SPEAR.
This Spear, Dear Lord, that's dyd with Blood of thine
Pierces my Heart with Wounds of Love divine.

The HARDNESS of the Heart.

Zech. vii. 12.

They made their hearts as hard as an adamant stone, lest they should hear the law.

EPIG. 8.

WORDS move thee not, nor gifts, nor strokes:
Thy sturdy adamantine heart provokes
My justice, slights my mercies: anvil-like,
Thou stand'st unmoved, though my hammer strike.

ODE VIII.

1.

What have we here? An heart? It looks like one,
 The shape and colour speak it such:
 But, having brought it to the touch,
I find it is no better than a stone.
  Adamants are
  Softer by far.

2.

Long hath it steeped been in Mercy's milk,
 And soaked in Salvation,
 Meet for the alteration
Of anvils, to have made them soft as silk;
  Yet it is still
  Harden'd in ill.

Oft

3.

Oft have I rain'd my word upon it, oft
   The dew of heaven hath diftill'd,
   With promifes of mercy fill'd,
Able to make mountains of marble foft :
     Yet it is not
     Changed a jot.

4.

My beams of love fhine on it every day,
   Able to thaw the thickeft ice ;
   And, where they enter in a trice,
To make congealed chryftal melt away :
     Yet warm they not
     This frozen clot.

5.

Nay more, this hammer, that is wont to grind
   Rocks unto duft, and powder fmall,
   Makes no impreffion at all,
Nor dint, nor crack, nor flaw, that I can find :
     But leaves it as
     Before it was.

6.

Is mine almighty arm decay'd in ftrength ?
   Or hath mine hammer loft its weight ?
   That a poor lump of earth fhould flight
My mercies, and not feel my wrath at length,
     With which I make
     Ev'n heav'n to fhake!

7.
No, I am still the same, I alter not,
  And, when I please, my works of wonder
  Shall bring the stoutest spirits under,
And make them to confess it is their lot
    To bow or break,
    When I but speak.

8.
But I would have men know, 'tis not my word
  Or works alone can change their hearts;
  These instruments perform their parts,
But 'tis my Spirit doth this fruit afford.
    'Tis I, not Art,
    Can melt man's heart.

9.
Yet would they leave their customary sinning,
  And so unclinch the devil's claws,
  That keeps them captive in his paws,
My bounty soon should second that beginning:
    Ev'n hearts of steel
    My force should feel.

The DIVISION of the Heart.

Hof. x. 2.

Thine heart is divided. Now shall they be found faulty.

EPIG. 9.

*VAIN trifling virgin, I myself have giv'n
Wholly to thee: and shall I now be driv'n
To rest contented with a petty part,
That have deserved more than a whole heart?*

ODE IX.

1.

More mischief yet? was't not enough before
 To rob me wholly of thine heart,
  Which I alone
  Should call mine own,
 But thou must mock me with a part?
Crown injury with scorn, to make it more?

2.

What's a whole heart? Scarce flesh enough to serve
 A kite one breakfast: how much less,
  If it should be
  Offer'd to me,
 Could it sufficiently express
What I for making it at first deserve?

I gave 't

CORDIS DIVISIO.

*Me tibi cum totum dederim, vanissima, Cordis
Cur mihi, Virgo, tui pars aliquanta datur?*

The DIVISION of the HEART.

*Why dost thou give but half thine Heart to Me,
When my whole Self I offer'd up for Thee?*

THE SCHOOL OF THE HEART.

3.
I gave 't thee whole, and fully furnished
With all its faculties intire,
There wanted not
The smallest jot
That stricteft justice could require,
To render it completely perfected.

4.
And is it reason what I give in grofs
Should be return'd but by retale?
To take so small
A part for all,
I reckon of no more avail
Than, where I scatter gold, to gather drofs.

5.
Give me thine heart but as I gave it thee:
Or give it me at least as I
Have given mine
To purchase thine.
I halv'd it not when I did die;
But gave myself wholly to set thee free.

6.
The heart I gave thee was a living heart;
And when thy heart by sin was slain,
I laid down mine
To ransom thine,
That thy dead heart might live again,
And live intirely perfect, not in part.

7.
But whilst thine heart's divided, it is dead;
Dead unto me, unless it live
To me alone,
It is all one
To keep all, and a part to give:
For what's a body worth without an head?

8.
Yet this is worse, that what thou keep'st from me
Thou dost bestow upon my foes:
And those not mine
Alone, but thine;
The proper causes of thy woes,
From whom I gave my life to set thee free.

9.
Have I betroth'd thee to myself, and shall
The devil, and the world, intrude
Upon my right,
Ev'n in my sight?
Think not thou canst me so delude:
I will have none, unless I may have all.

10.
I made it all, I gave it all to thee,
I gave all that I had for it:
If I must lose,
I'd rather chuse
Mine interest in all to quit:
Or keep it whole, or give it whole to me.

CORDIS INSATIABILITAS.

Non triquetrum toto Cor est satiabile Mundo,
Solùm, quæ fecit Cor replet una Trias.

The INSATIABILITY of the HEART.

The World won't do; — Thy Heart's but empty still;
The Trinity must that Triangle fill.

The INSATIABLENESS of the Heart.

Hab. ii. 5.

Who enlargeth his defire as hell, and is as death, and cannot be fatisfied.

EPIG. 10.

THE whole round world is not enough to fill
  The heart's three corners, but it craveth ftill.
Only the Trinity, that made it, can
Suffice the vaft triangled heart of man.

ODE X.

1.

The thirfty earth and barren womb cry, Give:
  The grave devoureth all that live:
The fire ftill burneth on, and never faith,
  It is enough: The horfe-leech hath
Many more daughters: but the heart of man
Outgapes them all as much as heav'n one fpan.

2.

Water hath drown'd the earth: the barren womb
  Hath teem'd fometimes, and been the tomb
To its own fwelling iffue: and the grave
  Shall one day a fick furfeit have:
When all the fuel is confume'd, the fire
Will quench itfelf, and of itfelf expire.

3.
But the vaſt heart of man's infatiate,
    His boundleſs appetites dilate
Themſelves beyond all limits, his deſires
    Are endleſs ſtill; whilſt he aſpires
To happineſs, and fain would find that treaſure
Where it is not; his wiſhes know no meaſure.

4.
His eye with ſeeing is not ſatisfy'd,
    Nor's ear with hearing: he hath try'd
At once to furniſh ev'ry ſev'ral ſenſe,
    With choice of curious objects, whence
He might extract, and into one unite,
A perfect quinteſſence of all delight.

5.
Yet, having all that he can fanſy, ſtill
    There wanted more to fill
His empty appetite. His mind is vex'd,
    And he is inwardly perplex'd,
He knows not why: whenas the truth is this,
He would find ſomething there, where nothing is.

6.
He rambles over all the faculties,
    Ranſacks the ſecret treaſuries
Of art and nature, ſpells the univerſe
    Letter by letter, can rehearſe
All the records of time, pretends to know
Reaſons of all things, why they muſt be ſo.

                                              Yet

7.
Yet is not so contented, but would fain
  Pry in God's cabinet, and gain
Intelligence from heav'n of things to come,
  Anticipate the day of doom,
And read the issues of all actions so,
As if God's secret counsel he did know.

8.
Let him have all the wealth, all the renown,
  And glory, that the world can crown
Her dearest darlings with; yet his desire
  Will not rest there, but still aspire.
Earth cannot hold him, nor the whole creation
Contain his wishes, or his expectation.

9.
The heart of man's but little; yet this All,
  Compared thereunto, 's but small,
Of such a large unparallel'd extense
  Is the short-line'd circumference,
Of that three-corner'd figure, which to fill
With the round world, is to leave empty still.

10.
So, greedy soul, address thyself to Heav'n,
  And leave the world, as 'tis bereav'n
Of all true happiness, or any thing
  That to thine heart content can bring,
But there a tri-une God in glory sits,
Who all grace-thirsting hearts both fills and fits.

The RETURNING of the Heart.

Isaiah xlvi. 8.

Remember this, and shew yourselves like men : Bring it again to heart, O ye transgressors.

EPIG. II.

OFT have I call'd thee : O return at last,
Return unto thine heart : let the time past
Suffice thy wanderings : know that to cherish
Revolting still, is a mere will to perish.

ODE XI.

Christ.   1.
Return, O wanderer, return, return.
Let me not always waste my words in vain,
As I have done too long. Why dost thou spurn [again?
And kick the counsels that should bring thee back

The Soul.   2.
What's this that checks my course? Methinks I feel
A cold remissness seizing on my mind :
My stagger'd resolutions seem to reel,
As tho' they had in haste forgot mine heart behind.

Christ.   3.
Return, O wanderer, return, return.
Thou art already gone too far away,
It is enough : unless thou mean to burn
In hell for ever, stop thy course at last, and stay.

CORDIS REVERSIO.

Quum mihi jam toties revocata reverteris ad Cor:
Nolle redire, merum velle perire, puta.

The RETURNING of the HEART.

Not to return, so often call'd, will be
Thy certain Ruin; come, be rul'd by Me.

CORDIS EFFUSIO.

Vota quid occluso, quid Vulnera pectore celas?
Ante Deum fusi Cor natet instar Aquæ.

The POURING OUT of the HEART.

Thy Vows, and Wounds, conceal not in thy Breast;
Pour out thy Heart to God; He'll give thee rest.

THE SCHOOL OF THE HEART.

The POURING OUT of the Heart.

Lam. ii. 19.

Pour out thine heart like water before the face of the Lord.

EPIG. 12.

*WHY dost thou hide thy wounds? why dost thou hide
In thy close breast thy wishes, and so side
With thine own fears and sorrows? Like a spout
Of water, let thine heart to God break out.*

ODE XII.

The Soul.   1.
Can death, or hell, be worse than this estate?
Anguish, amazement, horror, and confusion,
Drown my distracted mind in deep distress.
My grief's grown so transcendent, that I hate
To hear of comfort, as a false conclusion
Vainly infer'd from feigned premises.
   What shall I do? what strange course shall I try,
   That, tho' I loathe to live, yet dare not die:

Christ.   2.
Be rule'd by me, I'll teach thee such a way,
As that thou shalt not only drain thy mind
From that destructive deluge of distress
That overwhelms thy thoughts, but clear the day,
And soon recover light and strength, to find
And to regain thy long-lost happiness.
   Confess, and pray. Say what it is doth ail thee,
   What thou would'st have, and that shall soon avail
                              [thee.

The Soul. 3.
Confess and pray? If that be all, I will.
Lord, I am sick, and thou art health, restore me.
Lord, I am weak, and thou art strength, sustain me.
Thou art all goodness, Lord, and I all ill.
Thou, Lord, art holy; I unclean before thee.
Lord, I am poor; and thou art rich, maintain me.
  Lord, I am dead; and thou art life, revive me.
  Justice condemns; let mercy, Lord, reprieve me.

4.
A wretched miscreant I am, compos'd
Of sin and misery; 'tis hard to say,
Which of the two allies me most to hell:
Native corruption makes me indispos'd
To all that's good; but apt to go astray,
Prone to do ill, unable to do well;
  My light is darkness, and my liberty
  Bondage, my beauty foul deformity.

5.
A plague of leprosy o'erspreadeth all
My pow'rs and faculties: I am unclean,
I am unclean: my liver broils with lust;
Rancour and malice overflow my gall;
Envy my bones doth rot, and keeps me lean;
Revengeful wrath makes me forget what's just:
  Mine ear's uncircumcis'd, mine eye is evil,
  And hating goodness makes me parcel * devil.

* *Parcel devil*; i. e. share or partake with him.

6.

My callous confcience is cauteriz'd;
My trembling heart fhakes with continual fear:
My frantick paffions fill my mind with madnefs:
My windy thoughts with pride are tympaniz'd:
My pois'nous tongue fpits venom every-where:
My wounded fpirit's fwallow'd up with fadnefs:
  Impatient difcontentment plagues me fo,
  I neither can ftand ftill, nor forward go.

7.

Lord, I am all difeafes: hofpitals,
And bills of mountebanks, have not fo many,
Nor half fo bad. Lord, hear, and help, and heal me.
Although my guiltinefs for vengeance calls,
And colour of excufe I have not any,
Yet thou haft goodnefs, Lord, that may avail me.
  Lord, I have pour'd out all my heart to thee:
  Vouchfafe one drop of mercy unto me.

The CIRCUMCISION of the Heart.

Deut. x. 16.
Circumcife the forefkin of your heart, and be no more stiff-necked.

EPIG. 13.

HERE, take thy Saviour's crofs, the nails and fpear,
That for thy fake his holy flefh did tear:
Ufe them as knives thine heart to circumcife,
And drefs thy God a pleafing facrifice.

ODE XIII.

1.

Heal thee? I will. But firft I'll let thee know
  What it comes to.
The plaifter was prepared long ago:
  But thou muft do
   Something thyfelf, that it may be
   Effectually apply'd to thee.

2.

I, to that end, that I might cure thy fores,
  Was flain, and dy'd,
By mine own people was turn'd out of doors,
  And crucify'd:
   My fide was pierced with a fpear,
   And nails my hands and feet did tear.

CORDIS CIRCUMCISIO.

Crux Capulum Chalybem Cultro dat Lancea, Clavi
Ferrum: hoc Cor circum-cide Deo-que sacra.

The CIRCUMCISION of the HEART.

The Cross, the Nails, the Spear, each give a part,
To form this Knife, to circumcise thine Heart.

3.
Do thou then to thyself, as they to me:
Make haste, and try,
The old man, that is yet alive in thee,
To crucify.
Till he be dead in thee, my blood
Is like to do thee little good.

4.
My course of physic is to cure the soul,
By killing sin.
So then thine own corruptions to controul
Thou must begin.
Until thine heart be circumcis'd,
My death will not be duly priz'd.

5.
Consider then my cross, my nails, and spear,
And let that thought
Cut rasor-like thine heart, when thou dost hear
How dear I bought
Thy freedom from the pow'r of sin,
And that distress which thou wast in.

6.
Cut out the iron sinew of thy neck,
That it may be
Supple, and pliant to obey my beck,
And learn of me.
Meekness alone, and yielding, hath
A power to appease my wrath.

7.
Shave off thine hairy scalp, those curled locks
  Powder'd with pride,
Wherewith thy scornful heart my judgments mocks,
  And thinks to hide
    Its thunder-threaten'd head, which bare'd
    Alone is likely to be spare'd.

8.
Rip off those seeming robes, but real rags,
  Which earth admires
As honourable ornaments, and brags
  That it attires;
    Which cumber thee indeed. Thy sores
    Fester with what the world adores.

9.
Clip thine ambitious wings, let down thy plumes,
  And learn to stoop,
Whilst thou hast time to stand. Who still presumes
  Of strength, will droop
    At last, and flag when he should fly.
    Falls hurt them most that climb most high.

10.
Scrape off that scaly scurf of vanities
  That clogs thee so:
Profits and pleasures are those enemies
  That work thy woe.
    If thou wilt have me cure thy wounds,
    First rid each humour that abounds.

CORDIS CONTRITIO.

In partes quam mille velim contundere Cor hoc,
Quod fuit auctori sponte rebelle suo.

The CONTRITION of the HEART.

In Thousand Pieces would I break this Heart,
Which leaves its Lord, and acts a Rebel's part.

The CONTRITION of the Heart.

Pſalm li. 17.

A broken and contrite heart, O God, thou wilt not deſpiſe.

EPIG. 14.

*HOW gladly would I bruiſe and break this heart
Unto a thouſand pieces, till the ſmart
Make it confeſs, that, of its own accord,
It wilfully rebell'd againſt the Lord!*

ODE XIV.

1.

Lord, if I had an arm or pow'r like thine,
    And could effect what I deſire,
    My love-drawn heart, like ſmalleſt wire
Bended and writhen, ſhould together twine
       And twiſted ſtand
       With thy command:
Thou ſhouldſt no ſooner bid, but I would go,
Thou ſhouldſt not will the thing I would not do.

2.

But I am weak, Lord, and corruption ſtrong:
    When I would fain do what I ſhould,
    Then I cannot do what I would:
Mine action's ſhort, when mine intention's long;
       Though my deſire
       Be quick as fire,

Yet my performance is as dull as earth,
And ſtifles its own iſſue in the birth.

3.

But what I can do, Lord, I will; ſince what
    I would, I cannot; I will try
    Whether mine heart, that's hard and dry,
Being calm'd, and tempered with that
        Liquor which falls
        From mine eye-balls,
Will work more pliantly, and yield to take
Such new impreſſion as thy grace ſhall make.

4.

In mine own conſcience then, as in a mortar,
    I'll place mine heart, and bray it there:
    If grief for what is paſt, and fear
Of what's to come, be a ſufficient torture,
        I'll break it all
        In pieces ſmall:
Sin ſhall not find a ſheard without a flaw,
Wherein to lodge one luſt againſt thy law.

5.

Remember then, mine heart, what thou haſt done;
    What thou haſt left undone: the ill
    Of all my thoughts, words, deeds, is ſtill
Thy curſed iſſue only: thou art grown
        To ſuch a paſs,
        That never was,
Nor is, nor will there be, a ſin ſo bad,
But thou ſome way therein an hand haſt had.

6.

Thou haſt not been content alone to ſin,
    But haſt made others ſin with thee;
    Yea, made their ſins thine own to be,
By liking, and allowing them therein.
        Who firſt begins,
        Or follows, ſins
Not his own ſins alone, but ſinneth o'er
All the ſame ſins, both after and before.

7.

What boundleſs ſorrow can ſuffice a guilt
    Grown ſo tranſcendent? Should thine eye
    Weep ſeas of blood, thy ſighs outvie
The winds, when with the waves they run at tilt *,
        Yet they could not
        Conceal one blot.
The leaſt of all thy ſins againſt thy God
Deſerves a thunderbolt ſhould be thy rod.

8.

Then ſince (repenting heart) thou canſt not grieve
    Enough at once while thou art whole,
    Shiver thyſelf to duſt, and dole †
Thy ſorrow to the ſeveral atoms, give
        All to each part,
        And by that art
Strive thy diſſever'd ſelf to multiply,
And want of weight with number to ſupply.

* *Run at tilt*; i. e. forcibly oppoſe. An antient martial exerciſe.
† *Dole*: i. e. deal out or divide.

The HUMILIATION of the Heart.

Eccles. vii. 9.

The patient in spirit is better than the proud in spirit.

EPIG. 15.

MINE heart, alas! exalts itself too high,
And doth delight a loftier pitch to fly
Than it is able to maintain, unless
It feel the weight of thine imposed press.

ODE XV.

1.

So let it be,
 Lord, I am well content,
And thou shalt see
 The time is not mis-spent,
Which thou dost then bestow, when thou dost quell
And crush the heart where pride before did swell.

2.

Lord, I perceive,
 As soon as thou dost send,
And I receive
 The blessings thou dost lend,
Mine heart begins to mount, and doth forget
The ground whereon it goes, where it is set.

In.

CORDIS HUMILLATIO.

Cor nimis heu! sese gaudens sublimibus effert.
Ni super impositum deprimat illud Onus.

The HUMILIATION of the HEART.

The Heart too high its lofty Pride would rear,
If not press'd down, and kept within its Sphere.

THE SCHOOL OF THE HEART. 51

3.

In health I grew
    Wanton, began to kick,
As though I knew
    I never should be sick.
Diseases take me down, and make me know,
Bodies of brass must pay the debt they owe.

4.

If I but dream
    Of wealth, mine heart doth rise
With a full stream
    Of pride, and I despise
All that is good, until I wake, and spy
The swelling bubble prick'd with poverty.

5.

A little wind
    Of undeserved praise
Blows up my mind,
    And my swoln thoughts doth raise
Above themselves, until the sense of shame
Makes me contemn my self-dishonour'd name.

6.

One moment's mirth
    Would make me run stark mad,
And the whole earth,
    Could it at once be had,
Would not suffice my greedy appetite,
Didst thou not pain instead of pleasure write.

Lord,

7.

Lord, it is well
    I was in time brought down,
Elſe thou canſt tell,
    Mine heart would ſoon have flown
Full in thy face, and ſtudy'd to requite
The riches of thy goodneſs with deſpite.

8.

Slack not thine hand,
    Lord, turn thy ſcrew about:
If thy preſs ſtand,
    Mine heart may chance ſlip out.
O queſt * it unto nothing, rather than
It ſhould forget itſelf, and ſwell again.

9.

Or if thou art
    Diſpos'd to let it go,
Lord, teach mine heart
    To lay itſelf as low
As thou canſt it: that proſperity
May ſtill be temper'd with humility.

10.

Thy way to riſe,
    Was to deſcend: let me
Myſelf deſpiſe,
    And ſo aſcend with thee.
Thou throw'ſt them down that lift themſelves on high,
And raiſeſt them that on the ground do lie.

* *Queſt*; i. e. ſqueeze.

CORDIS EMOLLITIO.

Cor, Marmor glaciale, Deus, ceu Cera liquescet,
Urere cum tuus hoc cœperit ignis Amor.

The SOFTENING of the HEART.

This Icy, Marble Heart, like Wax will melt,
Soon as the Fire of heavenly Love is felt.

THE SCHOOL OF THE HEART.

The SOFTENING of the Heart.

Job xxiii. 16.
God maketh my heart soft.

EPIG. 16.

MINE heart is like a marble ice,
Both cold and hard: but thou canst in a trice
Melt it like wax, great God, if from above
Thou kindle in it once thy fire of love.

ODE XVI.

1.

Nay, blessed Founder, leave me not:
   If out of all this grot
There can but any gold be got,
The time thou dost bestow the cost
   And pains will not be lost:
The bargain is but hard at most.
And such are all those thou dost make with me:
Thou know'st thou canst not but a loser be.

2.

When the sun shines with glitt'ring beams,
   His cold-dispelling gleams
Turn snow and ice to wat'ry streams.
The wax, so soon as it hath smelt
   The warmth of fire, and felt
The glowing heat thereof, will melt.
Yea, pearls with vinegar dissolve we may,
And adamants in blood of goats, they say.

If

3.

If nature can do this, much more,
　　Lord, may thy grace reſtore
Mine heart to what it was before.
　There's the ſame matter in it ſtill,
　　Though new inform'd with ill;
　　Yet can it not refiſt thy will.
Thy pow'r, that frame'd it at the firſt, as oft
As thou wilt have it, Lord, can make it ſoft.

4.

Thou art the Sun of righteouſneſs:
　　And though I muſt confeſs
Mine heart's grown hard in wickedneſs,
　Yet thy reſplendent rays of light,
　　When once they come in ſight,
　　Will quickly thaw what froze by night.
Lord, in thine healing wings a pow'r doth dwell,
Able to melt the hardeſt heart in hell.

5.

Although mine heart in hardneſs paſs
　　Both iron, ſteel, and braſs,
Yea, the hardeſt thing that ever was;
　Yet if thy fire thy Spirit accord,
　　And, working with thy word,
　　A bleſſing unto it afford,
It will grow liquid, and not drop alone,
But melt itſelf away before thy throne.

Yea,

6.

Yea, though my flinty heart be such,
 That the sun cannot touch,
 Nor fire sometimes affect it much,
 Yet thy warm reeking self-shed blood,
  O Lamb of God, 's so good,
  It cannot be withstood.
That aqua-regia of thy love prevails,
Ev'n where the pow'r of aqua-fortis fails.

7.

Then leave me not so soon, dear Lord,
 Though I neglect thy word,
 And what thy power doth afford;
 O try thy mercy, and thy love
  The force thereof may prove.
Soak'd in thy blood, mine heart will soon surrender
Its native hardness, and grow soft and tender.

56   THE SCHOOL OF THE HEART.

The Cleansing of the Heart.

Jer. v. 14.
O Jerusalem, wash thine heart from wickedness, that thou mayest be saved.

Epig. 17.

OUT of thy wounded Husband's, Saviour's side,
  Espoused soul, there flows with a full tide
*A fountain for uncleanness: wash thee there,
Wash there thine heart, and then thou need'st not fear.*

ODE XVII.

1.

O endless misery !
I labour still, but still in vain.
   The stains of sin I see
Are oaded * all, or dye'd in grain.
   There's not a blot
   Will stir a jot,
   For all that I can do.
   There is no hope
   In fullers' soap,
   Though I add nitre too.

2.

I many ways have try'd,
Have often soak'd it in cold fears ;
   And, when a time I spy'd,
Pour'd upon it scalding tears :

---

* *Oad*, or *Woad*, is a *deep* blue dye.

Have

CORDIS MUNDATIO.

Fons scaturit, lateris transfixi Vulnere Sponsi;
Hoc Cordis maculas abluc, Sponsa tui.

The CLEANSING of the HEART.

A Fountain flows from Jesu's wounded Side;
Here let the filthy Heart be purified.

Have rince'd and rubb'd,
And scrape'd and scrubb'd,
And turn'd it up and down:
  Yet can I not
  Wash out one spot;
It's rather fouller grown.

3.
    O miserable state!
Who would be troubled with an heart,
    As I have been of late,
Both to my sorrow, shame, and smart?
    If it will not
    Be clearer got,
  'Twere better I had none.
    Yet how should we
    Divided be,
  That are not two, but one?

4.
    But am I not stark wild,
That go about to wash mine heart
    With hands that are defile'd
As much as any other part?
    Whilst all thy tears,
    Thine hopes and fears,
  Both ev'ry word, and deed,
    And thought is foul,
    Poor silly soul!
  How canst thou look to speed?

5.
    Can there no help be had?
Lord, thou art holy, thou art pure:
    Mine heart is not so bad,
So foul, but thou canst cleanse it, sure.

[N° 10]   F   Speak,

Speak, bleſſed Lord,
Wilt thou afford
Me means to make it clean?
I know thou wilt:
Thy blood was ſpilt.
Should it run ſtill in vain?

6.
Then to that bleſſed ſpring,
Which from my Saviour's ſacred ſide
Doth flow, mine heart I'll bring;
And there it will be purify'd.
Although the dye,
Wherein I lie,
Crimſon or ſcarlet were;
This blood, I know,
Will make't as ſnow
Or wool, both clean and clear.

SPECULUM CORDIS.

Pro speculo Cordis, Cor aspice dulcis Jesu,
Imprimet hoc Cordi Vulnera viva tuo.

The MIRROR of the HEART.

Would'st thou inspect the Heart? Lord look at mine,
And let the Sight imprint new Wounds on Thine.

THE SCHOOL OF THE HEART.

The GIVING of the Heart.

Prov. xxiii. 26.
My son, give me thine heart.

EPIG. 18.

*THE only love, the only fear, thou art,
Dear and dread Saviour, of my sin-sick heart.
Thine heart thou gavest, that it might be mine:
Take thou mine heart, then, that it may be thine.*

ODE XVIII.

1.

Give thee mine heart? Lord, so I would,
And there's great reason that I should,
    If it were worth the having:
Yet sure thou wilt esteem that good,
Which thou hast purchas'd with thy blood,
    And thought it worth the craving.

2.

Give thee mine heart? Lord, so I will,
If thou wilt first impart the skill
    Of bringing it to thee:
But should I trust myself to give
Mine heart, as sure as I do live,
    I should deceived be.

3.
As all the value of mine heart
Proceeds from favour, not defert,
    Acceptance is its worth:
So neither know I how to bring
A prefent to my heav'nly King,
    Unlefs he fet it forth.

4.
Lord of my life, methinks I hear
Thee fay, that thee alone to fear,
    And thee alone to love,
Is to beftow mine heart on thee,
That other giving none can be,
    Whereof thou wilt approve.

5.
And well thou doft deferve to be
Both loved, Lord, and fear'd by me,
    So good, fo great thou art:
Greatnefs fo good, goodnefs fo great,
As paffeth all finite conceit,
    And ravifheth mine heart.

6.
Should I not love thee, bleffed Lord,
Who freely of thine own accord
    Laid'ft down thy life for me?
For me, that was not dead alone,
But defp'rately tranfcendent grown
    In enmity to thee?

THE SCHOOL OF THE HEART.

7.
Should I not fear before thee, Lord,
Whose hand spans heaven, at whose word
    Devils themselves do quake?
Whose eyes outshine the sun, whose beck
Can the whole course of nature check,
    And its foundations shake?

8.
Should I with-hold mine heart from thee,
The fountain of felicity,
    Before whose presence is
Fullness of joy, at whose right hand
All pleasures in perfection stand,
    And everlasting bliss?

9.
Lord, had I hearts a million,
And myriads in ev'ry one
    Of choicest loves and fears;
They were too little to bestow
On thee, to whom I all things owe,
    I should be in arrears.

10.
Yet, since my heart's the most I have,
And that which thou dost chiefly crave;
    Thou shalt not of it miss.
Although I cannot give it so
As I should do, I'll offer't though:
    Lord, take it, here it is.

The SACRIFICE of the Heart.

Pſalm li. 17.

The ſacrifices of God are a broken heart.

EPIG. 19.

NOR calves, nor bulls, are ſacrifices good
Enough for thee, who gav'ſt for me thy blood,
And, more than that, thy life : take thine own part,
Great God, that gaveſt all ; here, take mine heart.

ODE XIX.

1.

Thy former covenant of old,
Thy law of ordinances, did require
Fat ſacrifices from the fold,
And many other off'rings made by fire.
Whilſt thy firſt tabernacle ſtood,
All things were conſecrate with blood.

2.

And can thy better covenant,
The law of grace and truth by Jeſus Chriſt,
Its proper ſacrifices want
For ſuch an altar, and for ſuch a prieſt ?
No, no, thy goſpel doth require
Choice off'rings too, and made by fire.

A ſacrifice

CORDIS SACRIFICIUM.

Non Vituli cæcive Deo placet Hostia Tauri.
Cor mihi qui dedit, hic Cor sibi poscit Amor.

The SACRIFICE of the HEART.

God is not pleas'd with Calves or Bullocks slain:
The Heart He gave, is all He asks again.

3.
A sacrifice for sin indeed,
Lord, thou didst make thyself, and once for all:
So that there never will be need
Of any more sin-off'rings, great or small.
　The life-blood thou didst shed for me
　Hath set my soul for ever free.

4.
Yea, the same sacrifice thou dost
Still offer in behalf of thine elect:
　And, to improve it to the most,
Thy word and sacraments do in effect
　Offer thee oft, and sacrifice
　Thee daily, in our ears and eyes.

5.
Yea, each believing soul may take
Thy sacrificed flesh and blood, by faith,
　And therewith an atonement make
For all its trespasses: thy gospel faith,
　Such infinite transcendent price
　Is there in thy sweet sacrifice!

6.
But is this all? Must there not be
Peace-offerings, and sacrifices of
　Thankfgiving, tender'd unto thee?
Yes, Lord, I know I should but mock, and scoff
　Thy sacrifice for sin, should I
　My sacrifice of praise deny.

Bu

7.
But I have nothing of mine own
Worthy to be prefented in thy fight;
Yea, the whole world affords not one
Or ram, or lamb, wherein thou canft delight.
Lefs than myfelf it muft not be:
For thou didft give thyfelf for me.

8.
Myfelf, then, I muft facrifice:
And fo I will, mine heart, the only thing
Thou doft above all other prize
As thine own part, the beft I have to bring.
An humble heart's a facrifice,
Which I know thou wilt not defpife.

9.
Lord, be my altar, fanctify
Mine heart thy facrifice, and let thy Spirit
Kindle thy fire of love, that I,
Burning with zeal to magnify thy merit,
May both confume my fins, and raife
Eternal trophies to thy praife.

CORDIS PONDERATIO.

*Quod mihi donasti magno pro munere, non est
Si neget hoc justi ponderis æqua bilanx.*

The WEIGHING of the HEART.

*This Gift of thine will not appear so great,
Unless when tried it proves of proper Weight.*

The WEIGHING of the Heart.

Prov. xxi. 2.

The Lord pondereth the heart.

EPIG. 20.

THE heart thou giv'ſt as a great gift, my love,
Brought to the trial, nothing ſuch will prove ;
If juſtice' equal balance tell thy fight,
That, weighed with my law, it is too light.

ODE XX.

1.

'Tis true, indeed, an heart,
Such as it ought to be,
Intire and found in ev'ry part,
Is always welcome unto me.
He that would pleaſe me with an offering,
Cannot a better have, altho' he were a king.

2.

And there is none ſo poor,
But, if he will, he may
Bring me an heart, altho' no more,
And on mine altar may it lay.
The ſacrifice which I like beſt, is ſuch
As rich men cannot boaſt, and poor men need not
[grutch.

Yet

3.
Yet ev'ry heart is not
A gift sufficient,
It must be purge'd from ev'ry spot,
And all to pieces must be rent.
Tho' thou hast sought to circumcise, and bruise 't,
It must be weighed too, or else I shall refuse 't.

4.
My balances are just,
My law's an equal weight;
The beam is strong, and thou may'st trust
My steady hand to hold it streight.
Were thine heart equal to the world in sight,
Yet it were nothing worth, if it should prove too light.

5.
And so thou seest it doth;
My pond'rous law doth press
This scale; but that, as fill'd with froth,
Tilts up, and makes no shew of stress.
Thine heart is empty sure, or else it would
In weight, as well as bulk, better proportion hold.

6.
Search it, and thou shalt find
It wants integrity;
And yet is not so thorough line'd
With single-eye'd sincerity,
As it should be: some more humility
There wants to make it weight, and some more con-
[stancy.

Whilst

7.
Whilſt windy vanity
Doth puff it up with pride,
And double-face'd hypocriſy
Doth many empty hollows hide,
It is but good in part, and that but little,
Wav'ring unſtaidneſs makes its reſolutions brittle.

8.
The heart, that in my ſight
As current coin would paſs,
Muſt not be the leaſt grain too light,
But as at firſt it ſtamped was.
Keep then thine heart till it be better grown,
And, when it is full, I'll take it for mine own.

9.
But if thou art aſhame'd
To find thine heart ſo light,
And art afraid thou ſhalt be blame'd,
I'll teach thee how to ſet it right.
Add to my law my goſpel, and there ſee
My merits thine, and then the ſcales will equal be.

The TRYING of the Heart.

Prov. xvii. 3.

The fining-pot for silver, and the furnace for gold: but the Lord trieth the hearts.

EPIG. 21.

THINE heart, my dear, more precious is than gold,
Or the most precious things that can be told:
Provide first that my pure fire have try'd
Out all the dross, and pass it purify'd.

ODE XXI.

1.

What! take it at adventure, and not try
What metal it is made of? No, not I.
    Should I now lightly let it pass,
Take sullen lead for silver, sounding brass
    Instead of solid gold, alas!
What would become of it? In the great day
Of making jewels, 'twould be cast away.

2.

The heart thou giv'st me must be such a one,
As is the same throughout. I will have none
    But that which will abide the fire.
'Tis not a glitt'ring outside I desire,
    Whose seeming shews do soon expire:
But real worth within, which neither dross,
Nor base allays, make subject unto loss.

CORDIS PROTECTIO.

Ægide Cor magni mea Lux defende Laboris,
Quem pro Corde tuus ferre coegit Amor.

The DEFENCE of the HEART.

O Thou my Light and Life! thy Aid impart,
And let thy Sufferings now defend my Heart.

THE SCHOOL OF THE HEART.

3.

If, in the compofition of thine heart,
A ftubborn fteelly wilfulnefs have part,
    That will not bow and bend to me,
Save only in a mere formality
      Of tinfel-trimm'd hypocrify,
I care not for it, though it fhew as fair
As the firft blufh of the fun-gilded air.

4.

The heart that in my furnace will not melt,
When it the glowing heat thereof hath felt,
    Turn liquid, and diffolve in tears
Of true repentance for its faults, that hears
    My threat'ning voice, and never fears,
Is not an heart worth having. If it be
An heart of ftone, 'tis not an heart for me.

5.

The heart, that, caft into my furnace, fpits
And fparkles in my face, fall into fits
    Of difcontented grudging, whines
When it is broken of its will, repines
    At the leaft fuffering, declines
My fatherly correction, is an heart
On which I care not to beftow mine art.

6.

The heart that in my flames afunder flies,
Scatters itfelf at random, and fo lies
    In heaps of afhes here and there,
Whofe dry difperfed parts will not draw near
    To one another, and adhere
In a firm union, hath no metal in't

7.
The heart that vapours out itself in smoak,
And with those cloudy shadows thinks to cloak
    Its empty nakedness, how much
Soever thou esteemest it, is such
    As never will endure my touch.
Before I take't for mine, then I will try
What kind of metal in thine heart doth lie.

8.
I'll bring it to my furnace, and there see
What it will prove, what it is like to be.
    If it be gold, it will be sure
The hottest fire that can be to endure,
    And I shall draw it out more pure.
Affliction may refine, but cannot waste
That heart wherein my love is fixed fast.

CORDIS SCRUTINIUM.

*Solus Ego immensam Cordis perscrutor Abyssum
Nautica quam potis est haud penetrare Bolis.*

The SEARCHING of the HEART.

*That which no Line can fathom, I alone
Can search: To Me the human Heart is known.*

THE SCHOOL OF THE HEART.

The SOUNDING of the Heart.

Jer. xvii. 9, 10.

The heart is deceitful above all things, and desperately wicked; who can know it? I the Lord.

EPIG. 22.

I, *THAT alone am infinite, can try*
How deep within itself thine heart doth lie.
Thy seaman's plummet can but reach the ground:
I find that which thine heart itself ne'er found.

ODE XXII.

1.

A goodly heart to see to, fair and fat!
    It may be so: and what of that?
Is it not hollow? Hath it not within
    A bottomless whirlpool of sin?
Are there not secret creeks and crannies there,
    Turning and winding corners, where
The heart itself ev'n from itself may hide,
    And lurk in secret unespy'd?
I'll none of it, if such a one it prove:
Truth in the inward parts is that I love.

2.

But who can tell what is within thine heart?
    'Tis not a work of nature, art
Cannot perform that task: 'tis I alone,
    Not man, to whom man's heart is known.

Sound it thou may'st, and must: but then the line
    And plummet must be mine, not thine;
And I must guide it too, thine hand and eye
    May quickly be deceiv'd: but I,
That made thine heart at first, am better skill'd
To know when it is empty, when 'tis fill'd.

3.

Lest then thou should'st deceive thyself, for Me
    Thou canst not; I will let thee see
Some of those depths of Satan, depths of hell,
    Wherewith thine hollow heart doth swell.
Under pretence of knowledge in thy mind,
    Error and ignorance I find;
Quicksands of rotten superstition,
    Spread over with misprision *.
Some things thou knowest not, mis-knowest others,
And oft thy conscience its own knowledge smothers.

4.

Thy crooked will, that seemingly inclines
    To follow reason's dictates, twines
Another way in secret, leaves its guide,
    And lags behind, or swerves aside:
Crab-like, creeps backward; when it should have made
    Progress in good, is retrograde.
Whilst it pretends a privilege above
    Reason's prerogative, to move
As of itself unmov'd, rude passions learn
To leave the oar, and take in hand the stern.

* *Misprision*; i. e. concealment of danger.

5.

The tides of thine affections ebb and flow,
    Rife up aloft, fall down below,
Like to the fudden land-floods, that advance
    Their fwelling waters but by chance.
Thy love, defire, thy hope, delight, and fear,
    Ramble they care not when, nor where,
Yet cunningly bear thee in hand, they be
    Only directed unto me,
Or moft to me, and would no notice take
Of other things, but only for my fake.

6.

Such ftrange prodigious impoftures lurk
    In thy præftigious * heart, 'tis work
Enough for thee all thy life-time to learn
    How thou may'ft truly it difcern:
That, when upon mine altar thou doft lay
    Thine off'ring, thou may'ft fafely fay,
And fwear it is an heart: for, if it fhould
    Prove only an heart-cafe, it would
Nor pleafing be to me, nor do thee good.
An heart's no heart, not rightly underftood.

* *Præftigious*; i. e. juggling.

The LEVELLING of the Heart.

Pſalm xcvii. 11.
Gladneſs for the upright in heart.

EPIG. 23.

SET thine heart upright, if thou would'ſt rejoice,
And pleaſe thyſelf in thine heart's pleaſing choice:
But then be ſure thy plumb and level be.
Rightly apply'd to that which pleaſeth me.

ODE XXIII.

1.

Nay, yet I have not done: one trial more
Thine heart muſt undergo, before
I will accept of it:
Unleſs I ſee
It upright be,
I cannot think it fit
To be admitted in my ſight,
And to partake of mine eternal light.

2.

My will's the rule of righteouſneſs, as free
From error as uncertainty:
What I would have is juſt.
Thou muſt deſire
What I require,
And take it upon truſt:
If thou prefer thy will to mine,
The level's loſt, and thou go'ſt out of line.

Emb. 23.

CORDIS RECTIFICATIO.

Ad rectum persæpe mei Cor Cordis amufsim.
Si rectum cupias exige Nula tuum.

The LEVELLING of the HEART.

The Heart's true Level if you still design,
Then often bring it to be try'd by mine.

3.

Canst thou not see how thine heart turns aside,
And leans toward thyself? How wide
   A distance there is here?.
     Until I see
     Both sides agree
   Alike with mine, 'tis clear
The middle is not where 't should be;
Likes something better, though it look at me.

4.

I, that know best how to dispose of thee,
   Would have thy portion poverty,
     Lest wealth should make thee proud,
     And me forget:
     But thou hast set
   Thy voice to cry aloud
For riches; and unless I grant
All that thou wishest, thou complain'st of want.

5.

I, to preserve thine health, would have thee fast
   From nature's dainties, lest at last
     Thy senses sweet delight
     Should end in smart:
     But thy vain heart
   Will have its appetite
Pleased to-day, though grief and sorrow
Threaten to cancel all thy joys to-morrow.

6.

I, to prevent thy hurt by climbing high,
    Would have thee be content to lie
    Quiet and safe below,
        Where peace doth dwell;
        But thou doft fwell
    With vaft defires, as though
    A little blaft of vulgar breath
Were better than deliverance from death.

7.

I, to procure thy happinefs, would have
    Thee mercy at mine hands to crave:
    But thou doft merit plead,
        And wilt have none
        But of thine own,
    Till juftice ftrike thee dead.
And all thy crooked paths go crofs to mine.

Emb. 24.

CORDIS RENOVATIO.

Cum nova cuncta placent, Vetus O Cor!pone Novumque,
Quod tibi pro veteri Sponsa repono Cape.

The RENEWING of the HEART.

Since so much Pleasure Novelties impart,
Resign thine Old, for this New, Better Heart.

THE SCHOOL OF THE HEART.

The RENEWING of the Heart.

Ezek. xxxvi. 26.

A new heart will I give you, and a new spirit will I put within you.

EPIG. 24.

ART thou delighted with strange novelties,
Which often prove but old fresh-garnish'd lyes?
Leave then thine old, take the new heart I give thee:
Condemn thyself, that so I may reprieve thee.

ODE XXIV.

1.

No, no, I fee
There is no remedy;
An heart, that wants both weight and worth,
That's fill'd with nought but empty hollowness,
And screw'd aside with stubborn wilfulness,
   Is only fit to be cast forth,
     Nor to be given me,
     Nor kept by thee.

2.

Then let it go;
And if thou wilt bestow
An acceptable heart on me,
I'll furnish thee with one shall serve the turn
Both to be kept and given: which will burn
   With zeal, yet not consumed be:
     Nor with a scornful eye
     Blast standers-by.

3.

The heart, that I
Will give thee, though it lie
Bury'd in seas of sorrows, yet
Will not be drown'd with doubt, or difcontent,
Though fad complaints fometimes may give a vent
To grief, and tears the cheeks may wet,
Yet it exceeds their art
To hurt his heart.

4.

The heart I give,
Though it defire to live,
And bathe itfelf in all content,
Yet will not toil, or taint itfelf with any:
Although it take a view and tafte of many,
It feeds on few, as though it meant
To breakfaft only here,
And dine elfewhere.

5.

This heart is frefh
And new: an heart of flefh,
Not, as thine old one was, of ftone.
A lively fp'ritly heart, and moving ftill,
Active to what is good, but flow to ill:
An heart, that with a figh and groan
Can blaft all worldly joys,
As trifling toys.

6.

This heart is found,
And folid will be found;
'Tis not an empty airy flafh,
That baits at butterflies, and with full cry
Opens at ev'ry flirting vanity.
It flights and fcorns fuch paltry trafh:
But for eternity
Dares live or die.

7.

I know thy mind:
Thou feek'ft content to find
In fuch things as are new and ftrange.
Wander no further then: lay by thine old,
Take the new heart I give thee, and be bold
To boaft thyfelf of the exchange,
And fay, that a new heart
Exceeds all art.

The ENLIGHTENING of the Heart.

Pſalm xxxiv. 5.

They looked on him, and were lightened.

EPIG. 25.

*THOU that art Light of lights, the only ſight
Of the blind world, lend me thy ſaving light:
Diſperſe thoſe miſts which in my ſoul have made
Darkneſs as deep as hell's eternal ſhade.*

ODE XXV.

1.

Alas! that I
Could not before eſpy
The ſoul-confounding miſery
Of this more than Egyptian dreadful night!
To be deprived of the light,
And to have eyes, but eyes devoid of ſight,
As mine have been, is ſuch a woe,
As he alone can know
That feels it ſo.

2.

Darkneſs has been
My God and me between,
Like an opacous doubled ſcreen,
Thro' which nor light nor heat could paſſage find,
Groſs ignorance hath made my mind
And underſtanding not clear-eye'd, but blind;
My will to all that's good is cold,
Nor can I, thou I would,
Do what I ſhould.—

No,

CORDIS ILLUMINATIO.

*Lux de luce, Deus, cæci Lux unica Mundi,
Corde graves tenebras discute luce tua.*

The ENLIGHTENING of the HEART.

*Thou Light of Lights, O by thy Presence bright
Chace my Heart's Darkness, and impart thy Light.*

THE SCHOOL OF THE HEART.

3.
No, now I see
There is no remedy
Left in myself: it cannot be
That blind men in the dark should find the way
To blessedness: although they may
Imagine the high midnight is noon day,
As I have done till now, they'll know
At last, unto their woe,
'Twas nothing so.

4.
Now I perceive
Presumption doth bereave
Men of all hope of help, and leave
Them, as it finds them, drown'd in misery:
Despairing of themselves, to cry
For mercy, is the only remedy
That sin-sick souls can have; to pray
Against this darkness, may
Turn it to day.

5.
Then unto thee,
Great Lord of light, let me
Direct my prayer, that I may see.
Thou, that didst make mine eyes, canst soon restore
That pow'r of sight they had before,
And, if thou seest it good, canst give them more.
The night will quickly shine like day,
If thou do but display
One glorious ray.

I must

6.
I must confess,
And I can do no less,
Thou art the Sun of righteousness:
There's healing in thy wings; thy light is life;
My darkness death. To end all strife,
Be thou mine husband, let me be thy wife.
So light and life divine
Will all be thine.

CORDIS TABULA LEGES.

Scribe novam, teneri nunc Cordis in æquore Legem,
Cum vetus in duris sit mihi scripta petris.

The LAW-TABLE of the HEART.

Leave the Stone Tables for thy Saviour's part,
Keep Thou the Law that's written in thy Heart.

The TABLE of the Heart.

Jer. xxxi. 33.
I will put my law in their inward parts, and write it in their hearts.

EPIG. 26.

IN the soft table of thine heart I'll write
A new law, which I will newly indite.
Hard stony tables did contain the old:
But tender leaves of flesh shall this infold.

ODE XXVI.

1.

What will thy sight
Avail thee, or my light,
If there be nothing in thine heart to see
Acceptable to me?
A self-writ heart will not
Please me, or do thee any good; I wot,
The paper must be thine,
The writing mine.

2.

What I indite
'Tis I alone can write,
And write in books that I myself have made.
'Tis not an easy trade,
To read or write in hearts:
They that are skilful in all other arts,
When they take this in hand,
Are at a stand.

3.

My law of old
Tables of stone did hold,
Wherein I wrote what I before had spoken,
Yet were they quickly broken:
A sign the covenant
Contain'd in them would due observance want.
Nor did they long remain
Copy'd again.

4.

But now I'll try
What force in flesh doth lie:
Whether thine heart renew'd afford a place
Fit for my law of grace.
This covenant is better
Than that, though glorious, of the killing letter;
This gives life, not by merit,
But by my Spirit.

5.

When in men's hearts,
And their most inward parts,
I by my Spirit write my law of love,
They then begin to move,
Not by themselves, but me,
And their obedience is their liberty.
There are no slaves, but those
That serve their foes.

6.

When I have writ
My covenant in it,
View thine heart by my light, and thou shalt see
A present fit for me.
The worth, for which I look,
Lies in the lines, not in the leaves of th' book.
Coarse paper may be line'd
With words refine'd:

7.

And such are mine.
No furnace can refine
The choicest silver so, to make it pure,
As my law put in ure
Purgeth the hearts of men:
Which being rule'd, and written with my pen,
My Spirit, ev'ry letter
Will make them better.

The Tilling of the Heart.

Ezek. xxxvi. 9.

I will turn unto you, and ye shall be tilled and sown.

Epig. 27.

*MINE heart's a field, thy cross a plough; be pleas'd,
Dear Spouse, to till it, till the mould be rais'd
Fit for the feeding of thy word: then sow,
And if thou shine upon it, it will grow.*

ODE XXVII.

1.

So now methinks I find
Some better vigour in my mind;
My will begins to move,
And mine affections stir towards things above:
Mine heart grows big with hope; it is a field
That some good fruit may yield,
If it were till'd as it should be,
Not by myself, but thee.

2

Great Husbandman, whose pow'r
All difficulties can devour,
And do what likes thee best,
Let not thy field, my heart, lie by, and rest;
Lest it be over run with noisome weeds,
That spring of their own feeds:
Unless thy grace the growth should stop,
Sin would be all my crop.

CORDIS ARATIO.

Cordis Agrum, crucis eja tuæ præscindat Aratrum,
Cui verbi inspergas Semina Sponse tui.

The TILLING of the HEART.

Lord, with thy Plow break up this Heart of mine,
And fit it to receive the Seed divine.

3.

Break up my fallow ground,
That there may not a clod be found
To hide one root of sin.
Apply thy plough betime : now, now begin
To furrow up my stiff and starvy heart;
No matter for the smart,
Although it roar, when it is rent,
Let not thine hand relent.

4.

Corruption's rooted deep,
Showers of repentant tears must steep
The mould, to make it soft :
It must be stirr'd, and turn'd, not once, but oft.
Let it have all its seasons. O impart
The best of all thine art:
For of itself it is so tough,
All will be but enough.

5.

Or, if it be thy will
To teach me, let me learn the skill
Myself to plow mine heart :
The profit will be mine, and 'tis my part
To take the pains, and labour, though th' increase
Without thy blessing cease :
If fit for nothing else, yet thou
May'st make me draw thy plough :

6.

Which of thy ploughs thou wilt,
For thou haft more than one. My guilt,
Thy wrath, thy rods, are all
Ploughs fit to tear mine heart to pieces fmall:
And when, in thefe, it apprehends thee near,
'Tis furrowed with fear:
Each weed, turn'd under, hides its head,
And fhews as it were dead.

7.

But, Lord, thy bleffed paffion
Is a plough of another fafhion,
Better than all the reft.
Oh faften me to that, and let the reft
Of all my powers ftrive to draw it in,
And leave no room for fin.
The virtue of thy death can make
Sin its faft hold forfake.

SEMINATIO IN COR.

Semina jam Terræ manda Divine Colone.
Ne nostri sterilis sit tibi Cordis Ager.

The SEEDING of the HEART.

With thine own hand, O Lord, now seed the Ground,
Lest this vile Heart be still unfruitful found.

THE SCHOOL OF THE HEART.

The SEEDING of the Heart.

Luke viii. 15.

That on the good ground are they, which, with an honest and good heart, having heard the word, keep it, and bring forth fruit with patience.

EPIG. 28.

*L*EST the field of mine heart should unto thee,
    Great Husbandman that made'st it, barren be,
Manure the ground, then come thyself and feed it ;
And let thy servants water it and weed it.

ODE XXVIII.

I.

Nay, blessed Lord,
    Unless thou wilt afford
Manure, as well as tillage, to thy field,
    It will not yield
That fruit which thou expecteft it should bear:
    The ground, I fear,
    Will still remain
Barren of what is good : and all the grain
    It will bring forth,
As of its own accord, will not be worth
    The pains of gathering
    So poor a thing.

Some

2.
Some faint defire,
That quickly will expire,
Wither, and die, is all thou canft expect.
If thou neglect
To fow it now 'tis ready, thou fhalt find
That it will bind,
And harder grow
Than at the firft it was. Thou muft beftow
Some further coft,
Elfe all thy former labour will be loft.
Mine heart no corn will breed.
Without thy feed.

3.
Thy word is feed,
And manure too: will feed,
As well as fill mine heart. If once it were
Well rooted there,
It would come on apace: O then neglect
No time: expect
No better feafon:
Now, now thy field mine heart is ready: reafon
Surrenders now,
Now my rebellious will begins to bow,
And mine affections are
Tamer by far.

4.
Lord, I have lain
Barren too long, and fain
I would redeem the time, that I may be
Fruitful to thee;

Fruitful

Fruitful in knowledge, faith, obedience,
    Ere I go hence:
    That when I come
At harvest to be reaped, and brought home,
    Thine angels may
My soul in thy celestial garner lay,
    Where perfect joy and bliss
    Eternal is.

5.

    If to intreat
    A crop of purest wheat,
A blessing too transcendent should appear
    For me to hear,
Lord, make me what thou wilt, so thou wilt take
    What thou dost make,
    And not disdain
To house me, though among thy coarsest grain;
    So I may be
Laid with the gleanings gathered by thee,
    When the full sheaves are spent,
    I am content.

The WATERING of the Heart.

Isaiah xxvii. 3.
I the Lord do keep it: I will water it every moment.

EPIG. 29.

*CLOSE downwards tow'rds the earth, open above,
Tow'rds heav'n, mine heart is. O let thy love
Distill in fructifying dews of grace,
And then mine heart will be a pleasant place.*

ODE XXIX.

1.

See how this dry and thirsty land,
Mine heart, doth gaping, gasping stand,
And, close below, opens tow'rds heav'n and thee.
Thou Fountain of Felicity,
Great Lord of living waters, water me:
Let not my breath, that pants with pain,
Waste and consume itself in vain.

2.

The mists, that from the earth do rise,
An heav'n-born heart will not suffice:
Cool it without they may, but cannot quench
The scalding heat within, nor drench
Its dusty dry desires, or fill one trench.
Nothing, but what comes from on high,
Can heav'n-bred longings satisfy.

See

CORDIS IRRIGATIO.

*Telluri clausum; Cælo patet: imphie rorem,
Cordis ab hoc varie flore virescet Humus.*

The WARTERING of the HEART.

*My Heart tow'rd Heav'n is open; let thy Showers
Gently distil, and aid the springing Flowers.*

THE SCHOOL OF THE HEART. 93

3.
See how the feed, which thou didſt ſow,
Lies parch'd, and wither'd; will not grow
Without ſome moiſture, and mine heart hath none
    That it can truly call its own,
By nature of itſelf, more than a ſtone:
    Unleſs thou water 't, it will lie
    Drowned in duſt, and ſtill be dry.

4.
    Thy tender plants can never thrive,
    Whilſt want of water doth deprive
Their roots of nouriſhment: which makes them call
    And cry to thee, great All in All,
That ſeaſonable ſhow'rs of grace may fall,
    And water them: thy word will do 't,
    If thou vouchſafe thy bleſſing to 't.

5.
    O then be pleaſed to unſeal
    Thy fountain, bleſſed Saviour; deal
Some drops at leaſt, wherewith my drooping ſpir'ts
    May be revived. Lord, thy merits
Yield more refreſhing than the world inherits:
    Rivers, yea ſeas, but ditches are,
    If with thy ſprings we them compare.

6.
    If not full ſhow'rs of rain, yet, Lord,
    A little pearly dew afford,
Begot by thy celeſtial influence
    On ſome chaſte vapour, raiſed hence
To be partaker of thine excellence:
    A little, if it come from thee,
    Will be of great avail to me.

7.
Thou boundlefs Ocean of grace,
Let thy free Spirit have a place
Within mine heart: full rivers, then, I know,
Of living waters, forth will flow;
And all thy plants, thy fruits, thy flow'rs will grow,
Whilſt thy ſprings their roots do nouriſh.
They muſt needs be fat, and flouriſh.

CORDIS FLORES.

Hæc tibi, nata tuo de semine conscero, Sponse,
Lilia, et his patriam floribus adde Solum.

The FLOWERS of the HEART.

These Lilies, rais'd from Seed which thou didst sow,
I give Thee, with the Soil in which they grow.

THE SCHOOL OF THE HEART.

The FLOWERS of the Heart.

Cant. vi. 2.

My Beloved is gone down into his garden, to the beds of spices, to feed in the gardens, and to gather lilies.

EPIG. 30.

THESE lilies I do consecrate to thee,
Beloved Spouse, which spring, as thou may'st see,
Out of the seed thou sowedst; and the ground
Is better'd by thy flow'rs, when they abound.

ODE XXX.

1.

Is there a joy like this?
What can augment my bliss?
If my Beloved will accept
A posy of these flowers, kept
And consecrated unto his content,
I hope hereafter he will not repent
The cost and pains he hath bestow'd
So freely upon me, that ow'd
Him all I had before,
And infinitely more.

2.

Nay, try them, blessed Lord;
Take them not on my word,
But let the colour, taste, and smell,
The truth of their perfections tell.
Thou that art infinite in wisdom, see
If they be not the same that came from thee.
If any difference be found,
It is occasion'd by the ground,
Which yet I cannot see
So good as it should be.

3.

What say'st thou to that Rose,
That queen of flowers, whose
Maiden blushes, fresh and fair,
Outbrave the dainty morning air?
Dost thou not in those lovely leaves espy
The perfect picture of that modesty,
That self-condemning shamefacedness,
That is more ready to confess
A fault, and to amend,
Than it is to offend?

4.

Is not this lily pure?
What fuller can procure
A white so perfect, spotless, clear,
As in this flower doth appear?
Dost thou not in this milky colour see
The lively lustre of sincerity,
Which no hypocrisy hath painted,
Nor self-respecting ends have tainted?
Can there be to thy sight
A more intire delight?

THE SCHOOL OF THE HEART.

5.

Or wilt thou have, befide,
Violets purple-dy'd?
The fun-obferving marigold,
Or orpin never waxing old,
The primrofe, cowflip, gilliflow'r, or pink,
Or any flow'r, or herb, that I can think
Thou haft a mind unto? I fhall
Quickly be furnifh'd with them all,
If once I do but know
That thou wilt have it fo.

6.

Faith is a fruitful grace,
Well-planted, ftores the place,
Fills all the borders, beds, and bow'rs,
With wholefome herbs and pleafant flow'rs:
Great Gardener, thou fay'ft, and I believe.
What thou doft mean to gather, thou wilt give.
Take, then, mine heart in hand, to fill't,
And it fhall yield thee what thou wilt.
Yea thou, by gath'ring more,
Shalt ftill increafe my ftore.

The Keeping of the Heart.

Prov. iv. 23.
Keep thy heart with all diligence.

Epig. 31.

LIKE to a garden that is closed round,
   That heart is safely kept, which still is found
Compass'd with care, and guarded with the fear
Of God, as with a flaming sword and spear.

ODE XXXI.

The Soul.   1.

Lord, wilt thou suffer this? Shall vermin spoil
   The fruit of all thy toil,
Thy trees, thine herbs, thy plants, thy flow'rs thus;
   And, for an overplus
Of spite and malice, overthrow thy mounds,
   Lay common all thy grounds?
Canst thou endure thy pleasant garden should
Be thus turn'd up as ordinary mould?

Christ.   2.

What is the matter? why dost thou complain?
   Must I as well maintain,
And keep, as make thy fences? wilt thou take
   No pains for thine own sake?
Or doth thy self-confounding fancy fear thee,
   When there's no danger near thee?
Speak out thy doubts, and thy desires, and tell me,
What enemy or can or dares to quell thee?

CORDIS CUSTODIA.

Quam bene conclusum Vigil hic Cor protegit hortum,
Præstricto munit quem Timor ense Dei.

The KEEPING of the HEART.

His Heart is guarded well, whose Hands appear
Arm'd with a flaming Sword, by Holy Fear.

The Soul.   3.

Many, and mighty, and malicious, Lord,
    That feek, with one accord,
To work my fpeedy ruin, and make hafte
    To lay thy garden wafte.
The devil is a ramping roaring lion,
    Hates at his heart thy Zion,
And never gives it refpite day nor hour,
But ftill goes feeking whom he may devour.

4.

The world's a wildernefs, wherein I' find
    Wild beafts of every kind,
Foxes, and wolves, and dogs, and boars, and bears;
    And, which augments my fears,
Eagles and vultures, and fuch birds of prey,
    Will not be kept away:
Befides the light-abhorring owls and bats,
And fecret-corner-creeping mice and rats.

5.

But thefe, and many more, would not difmay
    Me much, unlefs there lay
One worfe than all within, myfelf I mean,
    My falfe, unjuft, unclean,
Faithlefs, difloyal felf, that both entice
    And entertain each vice.
This home-bred traiterous partaking's worfe
Than all the violence of foreign force.

6.

Lord, thou may'st see my fears are grounded, rise
    Not from a bare surmise,
Or doubt of danger only, my desires
    Are but what need requires,
Of thy divine protection and defence
    To keep these vermin hence:
Which, if they should not be restrain'd by thee,
Would grow too strong to be kept out by me.

Christ.   7.

Thy fear is just, and I approve thy care.
    But yet thy comforts are
Provided for, ev'n in that care and fear:
    Whereby it doth appear
Thou hast what thou desirest, my protection
    To keep thee from defection.
The heart that cares and fears, is kept by me.
I watch thee, whilst thy foes are watch'd by thee.

CORDIS VIGILIA.

Te vigil exquirit Cor, dum Sopor occupat Artus,
Nec sine Te noctû, nec potis esse die.

The WATCHING of the HEART.

My wakeful Heart, that loves thy Presence, keeps
A constant Watch, e'en while my Body sleeps.

THE SCHOOL OF THE HEART.

The WATCHING of the Heart.

Cant. v. 2.

I sleep, but my heart waketh.

EPIG. 32.

*WHILST the soft bands of sleep tie up my senses,
My watchful heart, free from all such pretences,
Searches for thee, inquires of all about thee,
Nor day, nor night, able to be without thee.*

ODE XXXII.

1.

It must be so: that God that gave
Me senses, and a mind, would have
Me use them both, but in their several kinds.
Sleep must refresh my senses, but my mind's
A sparkle of heav'nly fire, that feeds
On action and employment, needs
No time of rest: for, when it thinks to please
Itself with idleness, 'tis least at ease.
Though quiet rest refresh the head,
The heart, that stirs not, sure is dead.

2.

Whilst, then, my body ease doth take,
My rest-refusing heart shall wake:
And that mine heart the better watch may keep,
I'll lay my senses for a time to sleep.

Wanton

Wanton defires fhall not entice,
Nor luft inveigle them to vice:
No fading colours fhall allure my fight,
Nor founds enchant mine ears with their delight:
I'll bind my fmell, my touch, my tafte,
To keep a ftrict religious faft.

3.

My worldly bufinefs fhall lie ftill,
That heav'nly thoughts my mind may fill:
My Martha's cumb'ring cares fhall ceafe their noife,
That Mary may attend her better choice.
That meditation may advance
My heart on purpofe, not by chance,
My body fhall keep holy day, that fo
My mind with better liberty may go
About her bufinefs, and ingrofs
That gain which worldly men count lofs.

4.

And though my fenfes fleep the while,
My mind my fenfes fhall beguile
With dreams of thee, dear Lord, whofe rare perfections
Of excellence are fuch, that bare infpections
Cannot fuffice my greedy foul,
Nor her fierce appetite controul;
But that the more fhe looks, the more fhe longs,
And ftrives to thruft into the thickeft throngs
Of thofe divine difcoveries
Which dazzle even angels' eyes.

Oh

5.

Oh could I lay aside this flesh,
And follow after thee with fresh
And free desires! my disentangled soul,
Ravish'd with admiration, should roll
   Itself and all its thoughts on thee,
   And, by believing, strive to see
What is invisible to flesh and blood,
And only by fruition understood,
   The beauty of each sev'ral grace,
   That shines in thy sun-shameing face.

6.

But what I can do that I will,
   Waking and sleeping, seek thee still:
I'll leave no place unpry'd into behind me,
Where I can but imagine I may find thee:
   I'll ask of all I meet, if they
   Can tell me where thou art, which way
Thou go'st, that I may follow after thee, [me.
Which way thou com'st, that thou may'st meet with
   If not thy face, Lord, let mine heart
   Behold with Moses thy back part.

The

CORDIS VULNERATIO.

Mille Cor hoc validis, mea Lux transfige sagittis,
Pharmaca sunt tua quæ Vulnera dextra facit.

The WOUNDING of the HEART.

With Thousand Shafts O pierce this Heart of mine;
The Wounds Thou givest, Lord, are Balm divine.

Let thy refplendent rays of knowledge dart
Bright beams of underftanding to mine heart,
　To my fin-fhadow'd heart, wherein
　　Black ignorance did firft begin
To blur thy beauteous image, and deface
The glory of thy felf-fufficing grace.

3.

Next let the fhaft of thy fharp-pointed pow'r,
Difcharged by that ftrength that can devour
　All difficulties, and incline
　　Stout oppofition to refign
Its fteelly ftubbornnefs, fubdue my will,
Make it hereafter ready to fulfil
　Thy royal law of righteoufnefs,
　　As gladly as, I muft confefs,
It hath fulfilled heretofore th'unjuft,
Profane, and cruel laws of its own luft.

4.

Then let that love of thine, which made thee leave
The bofom of thy Father, and bereave
　Thyfelf of thy tranfcendent glory
　　(Matter for an eternal ftory!),
Strike through mine affections all together,
And let that fun-fhine clear the cloudy weather,
　Wherein they wander without guide,
　　Or order, as the wind and tide
Of floating vanities tranfport and tofs them,
Till felf-begotten troubles curb and crofs them.

5.

Lord, empty all thy quivers, let there be
No corner of my spacious heart left free,
    Till all be but one wound, wherein
    No subtle sight-abhorring sin
May lurk in secret unespy'd by me,
Or reign in pow'r unsubdu'd by thee.
    Perfect thy purchas'd victory,
    That thou may'st ride triumphantly,
And, leading captive all captivity,
May'st put an end to enmity in me.

6.

Then, blessed archer, in requital, I
To shoot thine arrows back again will try;
    By pray'rs and praises, sighs and sobs,
    By vows and tears, by groans and throbs,
I'll see if I can pierce and wound thine heart,
And vanquish thee again by thine own art.
    Or, that we may at once provide
    For all mis-haps that may betide,
Shoot thou thyself, thy polish'd shaft, to me,
And I will shoot my broken heart to thee.

CORDIS INHABITATIO.

Spiritus, O mea Lux, cordis tuis incolat Ædem,
Sponse, ut amore tuo mi redameris amans.

The INHABITING of the HEART.

While here thy Spirit dwells, my Heart shall burn
With thine own Love; which sure thou wilt return.

The INHABITING of the Heart.

Gal. iv. 6.

God hath sent forth the Spirit of his Son into your hearts.

EPIG. 34.

MINE heart's an house, my Light, and thou canst tell
There's room enough, O let thy Spirit dwell
For ever there: that so thou may'st love me,
And, being lov'd, I may again love thee.

ODE XXXIV.

1.

Welcome, great guest, this house, mine heart,
    Shall all be thine:
    I will resign
Mine interest in ev'ry part:
Only be pleas'd to use it as thine own
For ever, and inhabit it alone:
There's room enough; and, if the furniture
Were answerably fitted, I am sure
    Thou would'st be well content to stay,
    And, by thy light,
    Possess my sight
With sense of an eternal day.

2.

It is thy building, Lord; 'twas made
    At thy command,
    And still doth stand
Upheld and shelter'd by the shade
Of thy protecting providence; though such
As is decayed and impaired much,

Since the removal of thy refidence,
When, with thy grace, glory departed hence:
It hath been all this while an inn
    To entertain
    The vile, and vain,
And wicked companies of fin.

3.

Although't be but an houfe of clay,
    Frame'd out of duft,
    And fuch as muft
Diffolved be, yet it was gay
And glorious indeed, when ev'ry place
Was furnifhed and fitted with thy grace:
When, in the prefence-chamber of my mind,
The bright fun-beams of perfect knowledge fhine'd:
When my will was thy bed-chamber,
    And ev'ry pow'r
    A ftately tow'r
Sweeten'd with thy Spirit's amber.

4.

But whilft thou doft thyfelf abfent,
    It is not grown
    Noifome alone,
But all to pieces torn and rent.
The windows all are ftopt, or broken fo,
That no light without wind can thorough go.
The roof's uncovered, and the wall's decay'd,
The door's flung off the hooks, the floor's unlay'd;
    Yea, the foundation rotten is,
    And every-where
    It doth appear
All that remains is far amifs.
                                                 But

5.

But if thou wilt return again,
    And dwell in me,
    Lord, thou shalt see
What care I'll take to entertain
Thee, though not like thyself, yet in such sort
As thou wilt like, and I shall thank thee for't.
Lord, let thy blessed Spirit keep possession,
And all things will be well: at least, confession
    Shall tell thee what's amiss in me,
      And then thou shalt
      Or mend the fault,
    Or take the blame of all on thee.

The ENLARGING of the Heart.

Psalm cxix. 32.

I will run the way of thy commandments, when thou shalt enlarge my heart.

EPIG. 35.

*HOW pleasant is that now, which heretofore
   Mine heart held bitter, sacred learning's lore!
Enlarged hearts enter with greatest ease
The straitest paths, and run the narrowest ways.*

ODE XXXV.

1.

What a blessed change I find,
  Since I entertain'd this guest!
Now methinks another mind
  Moves and rules within my breast.
    Surely I am not the same
    That I was before he came,
    But I then was much to blame.

2.

When, before, my God commanded
  Any thing he would have done,
I was close and gripple-handed,
  Made an end ere I begun.
    If he thought it fit to lay
    Judgments on me, I could say,
    They are good; but shrink away.

CORDIS DILATATIO.

Quam volupe est quod amare prius Cor duxit amarum,
Angustam late currere Corde Viam!

The ENLARGING of the HEART.

That's pleasant now, which once I strove to shun:
With Heart enlarg'd the narrow Way to run.

3.
All the ways of righteousnefs
 I did think were full of trouble;
I complain'd of tediousnefs,
 And each duty seemed double.
  Whilft I serv'd him but of fear,
  Ev'ry minute did appear
  Longer far than a whole year.

4.
Strictnefs in religion seemed
 Like a pined, pinion'd thing:
Bolts and fetters I esteemed
 More beseeming for a king,
  Than for me to bow my neck,
  And be at another's beck,
  When I felt my confcience check.

5.
But the cafe is alter'd now:
 He no sooner turns his eye,
But I quickly bend, and bow,
 Ready at his feet to lie:
  Love hath taught me to obey
  All his precepts, and to fay,
  Not to-morrow, but to-day.

6.
What he wills, I fay I muft:
 What I muft, I fay I will:
He commanding, it is juft
 What he would I fhould fulfill.
  Whilft he biddeth, I believe
  What he calls for, he will give.
  To obey him, is to live.

His

7.

His commandments grievous are not,
  Longer than men think them so :
Though he send me forth, I care not,
  Whilst he gives me strength to go.
    When, or whither, all is one,
    On his bus'ness, not mine own,
    I shall never go alone.

8.

If I be complete in him,
  And in him all fullness dwelleth,
I am sure aloft to swim,
  Whilst that Ocean overswelleth.
    Having Him that's All in all,
    I am confident I shall
    Nothing want, for which I call

CORDIS INFLAMMATIO.

Perge Amor, et succende mei penetralia Cordis,
Vivat ut in patrio ceu Salamandra rogo.

The INFLAMING of the HEART.

Thus my fond Heart, inflam'd with strong Desire,
Shall, like a Salamander, live in Fire.

The INFLAMING of the Heart.

Pſalm xxxix. 3.
My heart was hot within me: while I was muſing, the fire burned.

EPIG. 36.

*SPARE not, my Love, to kindle and inflame
Mine heart within throughout, until the ſame
Break forth, and burn: that ſo thy ſalamander,
Mine heart, may never from thy furnace wander.*

ODE XXXVI.

1.

Welcome, holy, heav'nly fire,
  Kindled by immortal love:
  Which, deſcending from above,
Makes all earthly thoughts retire,
    And give place
    To that grace,
Which, with gentle violence,
  Conquers all corrupt affections,
  Rebel nature's inſurrections,
Bidding them be packing hence.

2.

Lord, thy fire doth heat within,
  Warmeth not without alone;
  Though it be an heart of ſtone,
Of itſelf congeal'd in ſin,
    Hard as ſteel,
    If it feel

Thy

Thy diffolving pow'r, it groweth
  Soft as wax, and quickly takes
  Any print thy Spirit makes,
Paying what thou fay'ft it oweth.

3.

Of itfelf mine heart is dark;
  But thy fire, by fhining bright,
  Fills it full of faving light.
Though 't be but a little fpark
    Lent by thee,
    I fhall fee
More by it, than all the light,
  Which in fulleft meafures ftreams
  From corrupted nature's beams,
Can difcover to my fight.

4.

Though mine heart be ice and fnow
  To the things which thou haft chofen,
  All benumb'd with cold, and frozen,
Yet thy fire will make it glow.
    Though it burns,
    When it turns
Tow'rds the things which thou doft hate:
  Yet thy bleffed warmth, no doubt,
  Will that wild-fire foon draw out,
And the heat thereof abate.

5.

Lord, thy fire is active, ufing
  Always either to afcend
  To its native heav'n, or lend
Heat to others: and diffufing

Of its store,
Gathers more,
Never ceasing till it make
All things like itself, and longing
To see others come with thronging
Of thy goodness to partake.

6.

Lord, then let thy fire inflame
My cold heart so thoroughly,
That the heat may never die,
But continue still the same:
That I may
Ev'ry day
More and more, consuming sin,
Kindling others, and attending
All occasions of ascending,
Heaven upon earth begin.

The LADDER of the Heart.

Psalm lxxxiv. 5.

In whose heart are the ways of them.

EPIG. 37.

Wouldst thou, my love, a ladder have, whereby
Thou may'st climb heaven, to sit down on high?
In thine own heart, then, frame thee steps, and bend
Thy mind to muse how thou may'st there ascend.

ODE XXXVII.

The Soul.
1.
What!
Shall I
Always lie
Grov'ling on earth,
Where there is no mirth?
Why should I not ascend
And climb up, where I may mend
My mean estate of misery?
Happiness, I know, 's exceeding high:
Yet sure there is some remedy for that.

Christ.
2.
True,
There is.
Perfect bliss
May be had above:
But he, that will obtain
Such a gold-exceeding gain,
Must never think to reach the same,
And scale heav'n's walls, until he frame
A ladder in his heart as near as new.

CORDIS SCALÆ.

Vin' scalis Dilecta, poli conscendere Sedes?
Hic prius in proprio construe Corde gradus.

The LADDER of the HEART.

Would you scale Heav'n, and use a Ladder's aid?
Then in thy Heart let the first Step be made.

The Soul. 3.
Lord,
I will:
But the skill
Is not mine own:
Such an art's not known,
Unless thou wilt it teach:
It is far above the reach
Of mortal minds to understand.
But if thou wilt lend thine helping hand,
I will endeavour to obey thy word.

Christ. 4.
Well
Then, see
That thou be
As ready prest
To perform the rest,
As now to promise fair;
And I'll teach thee how to rear
A scaling-ladder in thine heart
To mount heaven with: no rules of art,
But I alone, can the compofure tell.

5.
First,
Thou must
Take on trust
All that I say;
Reason must not sway
Thy judgment crofs to mine,
But her sceptre quite refign.
Faith must be both thy ladder sides,
Which will stay thy steps whate'er betides,
And satisfy thine hunger, and thy thirst.

6.

Then,
The round
Next the ground,
Which I must see;
Is Humility:
From which thou must ascend,
And with perseverance end.
Virtue to virtue, grace to grace,
Must each orderly succeed in 'ts place;
And when thou hast done all, begin again.

CORDIS VOLATUS.

Quis mihi Chaonii geminas dabit alitis alas,
Pertæsum terræ, queis Cor ad Astra volet?

The FLYING of the HEART.

O that on Wings my weary Heart could rise,
Quit this vain World, and seek her native Skies!

The FLYING of the Heart.

Isaiah lx. 8.

Who are these that fly as a cloud, and as the doves to their windows?

EPIG. 38.

OH that mine heart had wings like to a dove,
That I might quickly hasten hence, and move
With speedy flight tow'rds the celestial spheres,
As weary of this world, its faults and fears.

ODE XXXVIII.

1.

This way, though pleasant, yet methinks is long:
  Step after step, makes little haste,
    And I am not so strong
      As still to last
       Among
      So great
    So many lets:
  Swelter'd and swill'd in sweat,
  My toiling soul both fumes and frets,
As though she were incline'd to a retreat.

2.

Corruption clogs my feet like filthy clay,
And I am ready still to slip:
Which makes me often stay,
When I should trip
Away.
My fears
And faults are such,
As challenge all my tears
So justly, that it were not much,
If I in weeping should spend all my years.

3.

This makes me weary of the world below,
And greedy of a place above,
On which I may bestow
My choicest love,
And so
Obtain
That favour, which
Excells all worldly gain,
And maketh the possessor rich
In happiness of a transcendent strain.

4.

What! must I still be rooted here below,
And riveted unto the ground,
Wherein mine haste to grow
Will be, though found,
But slow?
I know
The sun exhales
Gross vapours from below,
Which, scorning as it were the vales,
On mountain-topping clouds themselves bestow.

But

5.
But my fault-frozen heart is flow to move,
  Makes poor proceedings at the beft,
    As though it did not love,
      Nor long for reft
        Above.
        Mine eyes
      Can upward look,
    As though they did defpife
  All things on earth, and could not brook
Their prefence: but mine heart is flow to rife.

6.
Oh that it were once winged like the dove,
  That in a moment mounts on high,
    Then fhould it foon remove
      Where it may lie
        In love.
        And lo,
      This one defire
    Methinks hath imp'd it fo,
  That it already flies like fire,
And ev'n my verfes into wings do grow.

The UNION of the Heart.

Ezek. xi. 19.
I will give them one heart.

EPIG. 39.

*LIKE-minded minds, hearts alike heartily
Affected, will together live and die:
Many things meet and part: but love's great cable,
Tying two hearts, makes them inseparable.*

ODE XXXIX.

The Soul.   1.

All this is not enough: methinks I grow
More greedy by fruition: what I get
    Serves but to set
   An edge upon mine appetite,
   And all thy gifts do but invite
    My pray'rs for more.
Lord, if thou wilt not still increase my store,
Why didst thou any thing at all bestow?

Christ.   2.

And is't the fruit of having, still to crave?
Then let thine heart united be to mine,
    And mine to thine,
   In a firm union, whereby
   We may no more be thou and I,
    Or I and thou,
But both the same: and then I will avow,
Thou canst not want what thou dost wish to have.

CORDIS UNIO.

Unanimes Animæ, concordia vivite Corda,
Unum queis, velle et nolle, dat unus Amor.

The UNION of the HEART.

Live ye united Minds, and social Hearts,
To whom One Love but One Desire imparts.

The Soul. 3.

True, Lord, for thou art All in All to me;
But how to get my stubborn heart to twine
    And close with thine,
  I do not know, nor can I guess;
  How I should ever learn, unless
    Thou wilt direct
The course that I must take to that effect.
'Tis thou, not I, must knit mine heart to thee.

Christ. 4.

'Tis true, and so I will: but yet thou must
Do something tow'rds it too: First, thou must lay
    All sin away,
  And separate from that, which would
  Our meeting intercept, and hold
    Us distant still:
I am all goodness, and can close with ill
No more than richest diamonds with dust.

5.

Then thou must not count any earthly thing,
However gay and gloriously set forth,
    Of any worth,
  Compare'd with me, that am alone
  Th' eternal, high, and holy One:
    But place thy love
Only on me and the things above,
Which true content and endless comfort bring.

Love

6.

Love is the loadstone of the heart, the glue,
The cement, and the folder, which alone
    Unites in one
  Things that before were not the same,
  But only like; imparts the name,
    And nature too,
Of each to th' other: nothing can undo
The knot that's knit by love, if it be true.

7.

But if in deed and truth thou lovest me;
And not in word alone, then I shall find
    That thou dost mind
  The things I mind, and regulate
  All thine affections, love, and hate,
    Delight, desire,
Fear, and the rest, by what I do require,
And I in thee myself shall always see.

CORDIS QUIES.

Mobile Cor nullâ potis est requiescere Sede,
Unus ei centrum nam Deus una Quies.

The REST of the HEART.

My Heart, of Earthly Scenes quite weary grown,
Seeks for Repose, and Rest, in God alone.

The REST of the Heart.

Pſalm cxvi. 7.

Return unto thy reſt, O my ſoul.

EPIG. 40.

MY buſy, ſtirring heart, that ſeeks the beſt,
Can find no place on earth wherein to reſt :
For God alone, the author of its bliſs,
Its only reſt, its only centre is.

ODE XL.

1.

Move me no more, mad world, it is in vain,
    Experience tells me plain
    I ſhould deceived be,
If ever I again ſhould truſt in thee.
    My weary heart hath ranſack'd all
    Thy treaſuries, both great and ſmall,
And thy large inventory bears in mind :
    Yet could it never find
    One place wherein to reſt,
Though it hath often tried all the beſt.

2.

Thy profits brought me loſs inſtead of gain,
    And all thy pleaſures pain :
    Thine honours blurr'd my name
With the deep ſtains of ſelf-confounding ſhame.

Thy wifdom made me turn ftark fool,
And all the learning, that thy fchool
Afforded me, was not enough to make
Me know myfelf, and take
Care of my better part,
Which fhould have perifhed for all thine heart.

3.
Not that there is not place of reft in thee
For others: but for me
There is, there can be, none:
That God, that made mine heart, is he alone
That of himfelf both can and will
Give reft unto my thoughts, and fill
Them full of all content and quietnefs,
That fo I may pofîefs
My foul in patience,
Until he find it time to call me hence.

4.
On thee, then, as a fure foundation,
A tried corner-ftone,
Lord, I will ftrive to raife
The tow'r of my falvation, and thy praife.
In thee, as in my centre, fhall
The lines of all my longings fall.
To thee, as to mine anchor, furely ty'd,
My fhip fhall fafely ride.
On thee, as on my bed
Of foft repofe, I'll reft my weary head.

5.
Thou, thou alone, fhalt be my whole defire;
I'll nothing elfe require
But thee, or for thy fake.
In thee I'll fleep fecure; and, when I wake,

Thy

Thy glorious face shall satisfy
The longing of my looking eye.
I'll roll myself on thee, as on my rock,
  When threat'ning dangers mock.
Of thee, as of my treasure,
I'll boast and brag, my comforts know no measure.

6.

Lord, thou shalt be mine All; I will not know
  A profit here below,
  But what reflects on thee:
Thou shalt be all the pleasure I will see
  In any thing the earth affords.
  Mine heart shall own no words
Of honour, out of which I cannot raise
  The matter of thy praise.
  Nay, I will not be mine,
Unless thou wilt vouchsafe to have me thine.

The

The BATHING of the Heart.

Joel iii. 21.

I will cleanse their blood, that I have not cleansed.

EPIG. 41.

THIS bath thy Saviour swet with drops of blood,
Sick heart, of purpose for to do thee good.
They that have try'd it can the virtue tell;
Come, then, and use it, if thou wilt be well.

ODE XLI.

1.

All this thy God hath done for thee:
    And now, mine heart,
It is high time that thou should'st be
    Acting thy part,
And meditating on his blessed passion,
Till thou hast made it thine by imitation.

2.

That exercise will be the best
    And surest means,
To keep thee evermore at rest,
    And free from pains.
To suffer with thy Saviour, is the way
To make thy present comforts last for aye.

BALNEUM CORDIS EX SUDORE SANGUINEO.

Balnea sanguinei Sponsi sudata cruore,
Cor ægrum hic tibi quæ dat Paradisus Adi.

The BATHING of the HEART with the BLOODY SWEAT.
Christ's Bloody Sweat immortal Blessings gives,
As by its daily Sweat Man's Body lives.

THE SCHOOL OF THE HEART.

3.

Trace then the steps wherein he trod,
  And first begin
To sweat with him. The heavy load,
  Which for thy sin
He underwent, squeez'd blood out of his face,
Which in great drops came trickling down apace.

4.

Oh let not, then, that precious blood
  Be spilt in vain,
But gather ev'ry drop. 'Tis good
  To purge the stain
Of guilt, that hath defile'd and overspread
Thee from the sole of th' foot to th' crown of the head.

5.

Poison possesseth every vein,
  The fountain is
Corrupt, and all the streams unclean:
  All is amiss.
Thy blood's impure; yea, thou thyself, mine heart,
In all thine inward pow'rs, polluted art.

6.

When thy first father first did ill,
  Man's doom was read,
That in the sweat of's face he still
  Should eat his bread.
What the first Adam in a garden caught,
The second Adam in a garden taught.

7.

Taught by his own example, how
To sweat for sin,
Under that heavy weight to bow,
And never lin *
Begging releafe, till, with strong cries and tears,
The soul be drain'd of all its faults and fears.

8.

If sin's imputed guilt opprefs'd
Th' Almighty so,
That his sad soul could find no rest
Under that woe:
But that the bitter agony he felt
Made his pure blood, if not to sweat, to melt;

9.

Then let that huge inherent mafs
Of sin, that lies
In heaps on thee, make thee surpafs
In tears and cries,
Striving with all thy strength, until thou sweat
Such drops as his, though not as good as great.

10.

And if he think it fit to lay
Upon thy back
Or pains or duties, as he may,
Until it crack,
Shrink not away, but strain thine utmost force
To bear them chearfully without remorfe.

* *Lin*; i. e. linger, delay.

VINCULUM CORDIS EX FUNIBUS CHRISTI.

Crimina Te duro, fateor, mea fune ligarunt,
Dulcior astringat Cor Tibi funis Amor.

The BINDING of the HEART with the CORDS of CHRIST.

My Sins made Thee a cruel Bondage prove;
O bind my Heart to Thee with Cords of Love!

The Binding of the Heart.

Hof. xi. 4.
I drew them with cords of a man, with bands of love.

E P I G. 42:

MY sins, I do confess, a cord were found
Heavy and hard by thee, when thou waſt bound,
Great Lord of love, with them; but thou haſt twine'd
Gentle love-cords my tender heart to bind.

ODE XLII.

1.

What! could thoſe hands,
That made the world, be ſubject unto bands?
Could there a cord be found,
Wherewith Omnipotence itſelf was bound?
Wonder, mine heart, and ſtand amaz'd to ſee
The Lord of liberty
Led captive for thy ſake, and in thy ſtead.
Although he did
Nothing deſerving death, or bands, yet he
Was bound, and put to death, to ſet thee free.

2.

Thy ſins had ty'd
Thoſe bands for thee, wherein thou ſhould'ſt have dy'd:
And thou didſt daily knit
Knots upon knots, whereby thou made'ſt them fit
Cloſer and faſter to thy faulty ſelf.

Helpless and hopeless, friendless and forlorn,
  The sink of scorn,
And kennel of contempt, thou should'st have lain
Eternally enthrall'd to endless pain;

3.
  Had not the Lord
Of love and life been pleased to afford
  His helping hand of grace,
And freely put himself into thy place.
So were thy bands transferr'd, but not unty'd,
  Until the time he dy'd,
And, by his death, vanquish'd and conquer'd all
  That Adam's fall
Had made victorious. Sin, death, and hell,
Thy fatal foes, under his footstool fell.

4.
  Yet he meant not
That thou should'st use the liberty he got
  As it should like thee best;
To wander as thou listest, or to rest
In soft repose, careless of his commands:
  He that hath loos'd those bands,
Whereby thou wast enslaved to the foes,
  Binds thee with those
Wherewith he bound himself to do thee good,
The bands of love, love writ in lines of blood.

5.
  His love to thee
Made him to lay aside his majesty,
  And, cloathed in a vail
Of frail, though faultless flesh, become thy bail.
                                              But

But love requireth love: and since thou art
    Loved by him, thy part
It is to love him too: and love affords
    The strongest cords
That can be: for it ties, not hands alone,
But heads, and hearts, and souls, and all in one.

6.

    Come then, mine heart,
And freely follow the prevailing art
    Of thy Redeemer's love.
That strong magnetic tie hath pow'r to move
The steell'st stubbornness. If thou but twine
    And twist his love with thine;
And, by obedience, labour to express
    Thy thankfulness;
It will be hard to say on whether side
The bands are surest, which is fastest ty'd.

The Prop of the Heart.

Psalm cxii. 7, 8.

His heart is fixed, trusting in the Lord. His heart is established, he shall not be afraid.

Epig. 43.

*MY weak and feeble heart a prop must use,
But pleasant fruits and flowers doth refuse:
My Christ my pillar is; on him rely,
Repose, and rest myself, alone will I.*

ODE XLIII.

1.

Suppose it true, that, whilst thy Saviour's side
Was furrowed with scourges, he was ty'd
    Unto some pillar fast:
Think not, mine heart, it was because he could
Not stand alone, or that left loose he would
    Have shrunk away at last;
Such weakness suits not with Omnipotence,
Nor could man's malice match his patience.

2.

But, if so done, 'twas done to tutor thee,
Whose frailty and impatience he doth see
    Such, that thou hast nor strength
Nor will, as of thyself, to undergo
The least degree of duty or of woe,
    But would'st be sure at length

FVLCRVM CORDIS CHRISTI COLVMNA.

*Non Flores, non Poma, meum Cor debile poscit
Fulcire haec tua mi Christe Columna satis.*

CHRIST'S PILLAR the PROP of the HEART.

*Nor Fruits, nor Flow'rs, requires my weaken'd Heart;
Her Pillar, Christ, can lasting Aid impart.*

To flinch or faint, or not to stand at all,
Or in the end more fearfully to fall.

3.

Thy very frame and figure, broad above,
Narrow beneath, apparently doth prove
    Thou canst not stand alone,
Without a prop to bolster and to stay thee.
To trust to thine own strength, would soon betray thee.
    Alas! thou now art grown
So weak and feeble, wav'ring and unstaid,
Thou shrink'st at the least weight that's on thee laid.

4.

The easiest commandments thou declinest,
And at the lightest punishments thou whinest:
    Thy restless motions are
Innumerable, like the troubled sea,
Whose waves are toss'd and tumbled ev'ry way.
    The hound-pursued hare
Makes not so many doubles as thou dost,
Till thy cross'd courses in themselves are lost.

5.

Get thee some stay that may support thee, then,
And stablish thee, lest thou shoul'st start again.
    But where may it be found?
Will pleasant fruits or flow'rs serve the turn?
No, no, my tott'ring heart will overturn
    And lay them on the ground.
Dainties may serve to minister delight,
But strength is only from the Lord of might.

                             Betake

6.

Betake thee to thy Chrift, then, and repofe
Thyfelf, in all extremities, on thofe
  His everlafting arms,
Wherewith he girds the heavens, and upholds
The pillars of the earth, and fafely folds
  His faithful flock from harms.
Cleave clofe to him by faith, and let the bands
Of love tie thee in thy Redeemer's hands.

7.

Come life, come death, come devils, come what will,
Yet, faften'd fo, thou fhalt ftand ftedfaft ftill:
  And all the pow'rs of hell
Shall not prevail to fhake thee with their fhock,
So long as thou art founded on that Rock:
  No duty fhall thee quell,
No danger fhall difturb thy quiet ftate,
Nor foul-perplexing fears thy mind amate *.

  * *Amate*; i. e. difhearten.

COR PHIALA CHRISTO SITIENTI.

Respue quæ Judæ genus offert pocula fellis.
Compuncti Cordis sed libe Sponse merum.

The HEART a CUP to a THIRSTING CHRIST.

Refuse the Cup of Gall, O Spouse divine ;
But Wounded Hearts afford a pleasant Wine.

The SCOURGING of the Heart.

Prov. x. 13.
A rod is for the back of him that is void of understanding.

EPIG. 44.

*WHEN thou with-hold'st thy scourges, dearest Love,
My sluggish heart is slack, and flow to move:
Oh let it not stand still; but lash it rather,
And drive it, though unwilling, to thy Father.*

ODE XLIV.

1.

What do those scourges on that sacred flesh,
 Spotless and pure?
Must He, that doth sin-weary'd souls refresh,
 Himself endure
Such tearing tortures? Must those sides be gash'd?
 Those shoulders lash'd?
Is this the trimming that the world bestows
Upon such robes of Majesty as those?

2.

Is't not enough to die, unless by pain
 Thou antedate
Thy death beforehand, Lord? What dost thou mean?
 To aggravate

The guilt of sin, or to enhance the price
       Thy sacrifice
Amounts to? Both are infinite, I know,
And can by no additions greater grow.

3.

Yet dare I not imagine, that in vain
       Thou didst endure
One stripe: though not thine own thereby, my gain
       Thou didst procure,
That when I shall be scourged for thy sake,
       Thy stripes may make
Mine acceptable, that I may not grutch,
When I remember thou hast borne as much:

4.

As much, and more, for me. Come, then, mine
       And willingly   [heart,
Submit thyself to suffer: smile at smart,
       And death defy.
Fear not to feel that hand correcting thee,
       Which set thee free.
Stripes, as the tokens of his love, he leaves,
Who scourgeth ev'ry son whom he receives.

5.

There's foolishness bound up within thee fast:
       But yet the rod
Of fatherly correction at the last,
       If blest by God,

Will drive it far away, and wifdom give,
  That thou may'ſt live,
Not to thyſelf, but Him that firſt was ſlain,
And died for thee, and then roſe again.

6.

Thou art not only dull, and ſlow of pace,
  But ſtubborn too,
And refractory; ready to outface,
  Rather than do
Thy duty: though thou know'ſt it muſt be ſo,
  Thou wilt not go
The way thou ſhould'ſt, till ſome affliction
Firſt ſet thee right, then prick and ſpur thee on.

7.

Top-like thy figure and condition is,
  Neither to ſtand,
Nor ſtir thyſelf alone, whilſt thou doſt miſs
  An helping hand
To ſet thee up, and ſtore of ſtripes beſtow
  To make thee go.
Beg, then, thy bleſſed Saviour to transfer
His ſcourges unto thee, to make thee ſtir.

The HEDGING of the Heart.

Hosea ii. 6.
I will hedge up thy way with thorns.

E P I G. 45.

HE, that of thorns, would gather roses, may
In his own heart, if handled the right way.
Hearts hedge'd with Christ's crown of thorns, instead
Of thorny cares, will sweetest roses breed.

ODE XLV.

1.

A crown of thorns! I thought so: ten to one,
    A crown without a thorn, there's none:
There's none on earth, I mean; what, shall I, then,
    Rejoice to see him crown'd by men,
By whom kings rule and reign? Or shall I scorn
    And hate to see earth's curse, a thorn,
Prepost'rously preferr'd to crown those brows,
    From whence all bliss and glory flows?
      Or shall I both be glad,
        And also sad,
To think it is a crown, and yet so bad?

2.

There's cause enough of both, I must confess:
    Yet, what's that unto me, unless
I take a course his crown of thorns may be
    Made mine, transferr'd from him to me?

SEPIMENTUM CORDIS CORONA SPINEA.

Ne careat tua spina Rosis; Cor concolor armet ;
Horto arcet stygias Seps Diadema Feras.

The HEDGING of the HEART with a CROWN of THORNS
This Thorny Diadem, O Heart, behold ;
Thus Hedg'd, no Savage can approach the Fold.

Crowns, had they been of ſtars, could add no more
    Glory, where there was all before;
And thorns might ſcratch him, could not make him
    Than he was made, ſin and a curſe.   [worſe
      Come then, mine heart, take down
        Thy Saviour's crown
Of thorns, and ſee if thou canſt make 't thine own.

3.

Remember, firſt, thy Saviour's head was crown'd
    By the ſame hands that did him wound:
They meant it not to honour, but to ſcorn him,
    When in ſuch ſort they had betorn * him.
Think earthly honours ſuch, if they redound:
    Never believe they mind to dignify
      Thee, that thy Chriſt would crucify.
      Think ev'ry crown a thorn,
        Unleſs t' adorn
Thy Chriſt, as well as him by whom 'tis worn.

4.

Conſider, then, that as the thorny crown
    Circled thy Saviour's head, thine own
Continual care to pleaſe him, and provide
    For the advantage of his ſide,
Muſt fence thine actions and affections ſo,
    That they ſhall neither dare to go
Out of that compaſs, nor vouchſafe acceſs
    To what might make that care go leſs.
      Let no ſuch thing draw nigh,
        Which ſhall not ſpy
Thorns ready place'd to prick it till it die.

* *Betorn*; i. e. bemangled, torn in pieces.

5.

Thus, compafs'd with thy Saviour's thorny crown,
 Thou may'ft fecurely fit thee down,
And hope that he, who made of water wine,
 Will turn each thorn unto a vine,
Where thou may'ft gather grapes, and, to delight thee,
 Rofes : nor need the prickles fright thee.
Thy Saviour's facred temples took away
 The curfe that in their fharpnefs lay.
 So thou may'ft crowned be,
 As well as he,
And, at the laft, light in his light fhalt fee.

COMPUNCTIO CORDIS CLAVO TIMORIS DEI.

Hoc mihi Cor sancti Clavo transfige Timoris,
Pro Me, Qui Clavis in Cruce fixus eras.

The HEART PIERCED with the NAIL of GOD'S FEAR.

With Holy Fear let my Heart fastned be,
O Thou, once fastned to the Cross for me.

The FASTENING of the Heart.

Jer. xxxii. 40.

I will put my fear in their hearts, that they shall not depart from me.

EPIG. 46.

THOU, that waſt nailed to the croſs for me,
 Leſt I ſhould ſlip, and fall away from thee,
Drive home thine holy fear into mine heart,
And clinch it ſo, that it may ne'er depart.

ODE XLVI.

1.

What! doſt thou ſtruggle to get looſe again?
Haſt thou ſo ſoon forgot the former pain,
That thy licentious bondage unto ſin,
And luſt-enlarged thraldom, put thee in?
Haſt thou a mind again to rove, and ramble
Rogue-like a vagrant through the world, and ſcramble
For ſcraps and cruſts of earth-bred baſe delights,
And change thy days of joy for tedious nights
  Of ſad repentant ſorrow?
  What! wilt thou borrow
That grief to-day, which thou muſt pay to-morrow?

2.

No, ſelf-deceiving heart, leſt thou ſhould'ſt caſt
Thy cords away, and burſt the bands at laſt

Of thy Redeemer's tender love, I'll try
What further faftnefs in his fear doth lie.
The cords of love, foaked in luft, may rot,
And bands of bounty are too oft forgot:
But holy filial fear, like to a nail
Faften'd in a fure place, will never fail.
   This, driven home, will take
    Faft hold, and make
Thee that thou dareft not thy God forfake.

3.

Remember how, befides thy Saviour's bands,
Wherewith they led him bound, his holy hands
And feet were pierced, how they nail'd him faft
Unto his bitter crofs, and how at laft
His precious side was gored with a fpear:
So hard fharp-pointed ir'n and steel did tear
His tender flefh, that from thofe wounds might flow
The fov'reign falve for fin-procured woe.
   Then, that thou may'ft not fail
    Of that avail,
Refufe not to be faften'd with his nail.

4.

Love in a heart of flefh is apt to taint,
Or be fly-blown with folly: and its faint
And feeble fpirits, when it fhews moft fair,
Are often fed on by the empty air
Of popular applaufe, unlefs the falt
Of holy fear in time prevent the fault:
But, feafon'd fo, it will be kept for ever.
He that doth fear, becaufe he loves, will never
   Adventure to offend,
    But always bend
His beft endeavours to content his friend.

           Though

Though perfect love cast out all servile fear,
Because such fear hath torment: yet thy dear
Redeemer meant not so to set thee free,
That filial fear and thou should strangers be.
Though, as a son, thou honour him thy Father,
Yet, as a Master, thou may'st fear him rather.
Fear's the soul's centinel, and keeps the heart,
Wherein love lodges, so, that all the art
    And industry of those,
      That are its foes,
Cannot betray it to its former woes.

The NEW WINE of the Heart.

Pſalm civ. 115.

Wine that maketh glad the heart of man.

EPIG. 47.

*CHRIST the true vine, grape, cluſter, on the croſs
Trod the wine-preſs alone, unto the loſs
Of blood and life. Draw, thankful heart, and ſpare not:
Here's wine enough for all, ſave thoſe that care not.*

ODE XLVII.

1.

Leave not thy Saviour now, whate'er thou doſt,
 Doubtful, diſtruſtful heart;
Thy former pains and labours all are loſt,
 If now thou ſhalt depart,
And faithleſsly fall off at laſt from him,
Who, to redeem thee, ſpare'd nor life nor limb.

2.

Shall he, that is thy cluſter and thy vine,
 Tread the wine-preſs alone,
Whilſt thou ſtand'ſt looking on? Shall both the wine
 And work be all his own?
See how he bends, cruſht with the ſtraiten'd ſcrue
Of that fierce wrath that to thy ſins was due.

3.

Although thou canſt not help to bear it, yet
 Thruſt thyſelf under too,
That thou may'ſt feel ſome of the weight, and get,
 Although not ſtrength to do,
                                                    Yet

MUSTUM CORDIS E TORCULARI CRUCIS

En Cypri premitur botrus: Cor excipe grata,
De Torculari quæ Cruce Vina fluunt.

The NEW WINE of the HEART out of the PRESS of the CROSS
Behold, the Cyprian Clusters now are prest,
Accept the Wine, it flows to make Thee Blest.

Yet will to suffer something as he doth,
That the same stress at once may squeeze you bot

4.
Thy Saviour being prest to death, there ran
    Out of his sacred wounds
That wine that maketh glad the heart of man,
    And all his foes confounds.
Yea, the full-flowing fountain's open still
For all grace-thirsting hearts to drink their fill:

5.
And not to drink alone, to satiate
    Their longing appetites,
Or drown those cumbrous cares that would abate
    The edge of their delights;
But, when they toil, and soil themselves with sin,
Both to refresh, to purge, to cleanse them in.

6.
Thy Saviour hath begun this cup to thee,
    And thou must not refuse 't.
Press then thy sin-swoln sides, until they be
    Empty, and fit to use 't.
Do not delay to come, when he doth call;
Nor fear to want, where there's enough for all.

7.
Thy bounteous Redeemer, in his blood,
    Fills thee not wine alone,
But likewise gives his flesh to be thy food,
    Which thou may'st make thine own,
And feed on Him who hath himself reveal'd
The bread of life, by God the Father seal'd.

THE SCHOOL OF THE HEART.

8.
Nay, he's not food alone, but physic too,
    Whenever thou art sick ;
And in thy weakness strength, that thou may'st do
    Thy duty, and not stick
At any thing that he requires of thee,
How hard soever it may seem to be.

9.
Make all the haste, then, that thou canst to come;
    Before the day be past ;
And think not of returning to thy home,
    Whilst yet the light doth last.
The longer and the more thou draw'st this wine,
Still thou shalt find it more and more divine.

10.
Or if thy Saviour think it meet to throw
    Thee in the press again,
To suffer as he did ; yet do not grow
    Displeased at thy pain :
A summer season follows winter weather ;
Suff'ring, you shall be glorify'd together.

Revel. xxii. 17.

The Spirit and the Bride say, Come. And let him that heareth, say, Come. And let him that is athirst, come. And whosoever will, let him take the water of life freely.

The CONCLUSION.

IS this my period? Have I now no more
To do hereafter? Shall my mind give o'er
Its beſt employment thus, and idle be,
Or buſy'd otherwiſe? Should I not ſee
How to improve my thoughts more thriftily,
Before I lay theſe Heart-School lectures by?
Self-knowledge is an everlaſting taſk,
An endleſs work, that doth not only aſk
A whole man for the time, but challengeth
To take up all his hours until death.
Yet, as in other ſchools, they have a care
To call for repetitions, and are
Buſy'd as well in ſeeking to retain
What they have learn'd already, as to gain
Further degrees of knowledge, and lay by
Invention, whilſt they practiſe memory:
So muſt I likewiſe take ſome time to view
What I have done, ere I proceed anew.
Perhaps I may have cauſe to interline,
To alter, or to add: the work is mine,
And I may manage it as I ſee beſt,
With my great Maſter's leave. Then here I reſt
From taking out new leſſons, till I ſee
How I retain the old in memory.
And if it be his pleaſure, I ſhall ſay
Theſe leſſons before others, that they may
Or learn them too, or only cenſure me;
I'll wait with patience the ſucceſs to ſee.
And though I look not to have leave to play
(For that this ſchool allows not), yet I may
Another time, perhaps, if they approve
Of theſe, ſuch as they are, and ſhew their love
    To the SCHOOL OF THE HEART, by calling for't,
    Add other leſſons more of the like ſort.

The

THE LEARNING OF THE HEART.

The PREFACE.

I AM a scholar. The great Lord of love
And life, my tutor is; who, from above,
All that lack learning, to his school invites.
My heart's my pray'r-book, in which he writes,
Systems of all the arts and faculties:
First reads to me, then makes me exercise,
But all in paradoxes, such high strains
As flow from none but love-inspired brains:
Yet bids me publish them abroad, and dare
T' extoll his arts above all other arts that are.
Why should I not? methinks it cannot be.
But they should please others as well as me.
Come, then, join hands, and let our hearts embrace,
Whilst thus Love's labyrinth of arts we trace;
I mean the SCIENCES call'd Liberal:
Both Trivium and Quadrivium, sev'n in all.
  With the higher faculties, Philosophy;
  And Law, and Physic, and Theology.

The GRAMMAR of the Heart.

Psalm xv. 2.
That speaketh the truth in his heart.

MY Grammar, I define to be an art
  Which teacheth me to write and speak mine [heart;
By which I learn, that smooth-tongue'd flatt'ries are
False language, and, in love, irregular.
Amongst my letters, Vow-wells, I admit
Of none but Consonant to Sacred Writ:
And therefore when my soul in silence moans,
Half-vowel'd sighs and double deep-thong'd groans,
Mute * looks, and Liquid tears instead of words,
Are of the language that mine heart affords.
And, since true love abhors all variations,
My Grammar hath no moods nor conjugations,
Tenses, nor persons, nor declensions,
Cases, nor genders, nor comparisons:
Whate'er my Letters are, my Word's but one,
And, on the meaning of it, Love alone.
Concord is all my Syntax, and agreement
Is in my grammar perfect regiment.
  He wants no language that hath learn'd to love:
  When tongues are still, hearts will be heard above.

* *Mutes, liquids, diphthongs*; names of letters in the alphabet.

The RHETORIC of the Heart.

Pſalm xlv. 1.

My heart is inditing a good matter.

MY Rhetoric is not ſo much an art,
As an infuſed habit in mine heart,
Which a ſweet ſecret elegance inſtills,
And all my ſpeech with tropes and figures fills.
Love is the tongue's elixir, which doth change
The ordinary ſenſe of words, and range
Them under other kinds; diſpoſe them ſo,
That to the height of eloquence they grow,
Ev'n in their native plainneſs, and muſt be
So underſtood as liketh love and me.
When I ſay Chriſt, I mean my Saviour;
When his commandment, my behaviour;
For to that end it was he hither came,
And to this purpoſe 'tis I bear his name.
When I ſay, Hallow'd be thy name, he knows
I would be holy: for his glory grows
Together with my good, and he hath not
Given more honour than himſelf hath got.
So when I ſay, Lord, let thy kingdom come,
He underſtands it, I would be at home,
To reign with him in glory. So grace brings
My Love, in me, to be the King of kings *.
He teacheth me to ſay, Thy will be done,
But meaneth, he would have me do mine own,
By making me to will the ſame he doth,
And ſo to rule myſelf, and ſerve him both.

* That is, to be his love, or ſolely to him.

So

THE LEARNING OF THE HEART. 153

So when he faith, My fon, give me thine heart,
I know his meaning is, that I fhould part
With all I have for him, give him myfelf,
And to be rich in him from worldly pelf.
When he fays, Come to me, I know that he
Means I fhould wait his coming unto me;
Since 'tis his coming unto me that makes
Me come to him: my part he undertakes.
And when he fays, Behold I come, I know
His purpofe and intent is, I fhould go,
With all the fpeed I can, to meet him whence
His coming is attractive, draws me hence.
Thick-folded repetitions in love
Are no tautologies, but ftrongly move
And bind unto attention. Exclamations
Are the heart's heav'n-piercing exaltations.
Epiphonœma's and Apoftrophe's
Love likes of well, but no Profopope's.
Not doubtful but careful deliberations,
Love holds as grounds of ftrongeft refolutions.
Thus love and I a thoufand ways can find
To fpeak and underftand each other's mind;
And defcant upon that which unto others
Is but plain fong, and all their mufic fmothers.
Nay, that which worldly wit-worms call nonfenfe,
Is many times love's pureft eloquence.

The Logic of the Heart.

1 Pet. iii. 15.

Be ready always to give an answer to every man that asketh you a reason of the hope that is in you.

MY Logic is the faculty of faith,
    Where all things are resolv'd into, HE SAITH;
And ergo's, drawn from trust and confidence,
Twist and tie truths with stronger consequence
Than either sense or reason: for the heart,
And not the head, is fountain of this art.
And what the heart objects, none can resolve
But God himself, till death the frame dissolve.
Nay, faith can after death dispute with dust,
And argue ashes into stronger trust,
And better hopes, than brass and marble can
Be emblems of unto the outward man.
All my invention is, to find what terms
My Lord and I stand in: how he confirms
His promises to me, how I inherit
What he hath purchas'd for me by his merit.
My judgment is submission to his will,
And, when he once hath spoken, to be still.
My method 's, to be ordered by him;
What he disposeth, that I think most trim.
Love's arguments are all, I WILL, THOU MUST;
What He says and commands, are true and just.
  When to dispute and argue's out of season,
  Then to believe and to obey is reason.

F I N I S.

TRANSLATIONS OF THE LATIN MOTTO'S IN THE SCHOOL OF THE HEART.

ODE

I.   The *Infection* of the Heart.

WHILE Satan deceives thee with flatteirng baits, thy heart drinks in the deadly poison of disease and death.

II.   The *Taking away* of the Heart.

Lust pleases, and drunkenness please, and so the foolish mind grows stupid and dead; thus the heart is without heart.

III.   The *Darkness* of the Heart.

Oh the darkness of the heart! to which outer darkness will succeed, unless my light be a light unto you.

IV.   The *Absence* of the Heart.

How far, Oh fugitive! would thy heart flee? if thou canst be said to have an heart, who art neither mindful of me, nor of my self.

Translations of the Motto's in the SCHOOL ODE.

V.   The *Vanity* of the Heart.

The bellows of ambition blow up the vain heart with the wind of honors, whence it breathes nothing but a great nothing.

VI.   The *Oppreſſion* of the Heart.

Gluttony and drunkenneſs, two weights of ſolid lead, prevent our heaven-born hearts from mounting upwards.

VII.   The *Covetouſneſs* of the Heart.

Doſt thou inquire where thy heart is, heart-leſs wanderer? It is here, truly; even where that is which is dearer to thee than thy heart itſelf.

VIII.   The *Opening* of the Heart with the Spear.

The bleſſed ſpear, dyed red with the blood of Jeſus, pierces my heart with the wound of divine love.

IX.   The *Diviſion* of the Heart.

When I have given thee my whole ſelf, vain virgin, why is ſo ſmall a ſhare of thy heart given to me?

X.   The *Inſatiability* of the Heart.

Thy heart, which is a triangle, is not to be filled with the whole world: the Trinity, who made the heart, alone can ſatisfy it.

XI. The

Translations of the Motto's in the SCHOOL.

ODE

XI.   The *Returning* of the Heart.

Since now you have so often been exhorted by me to return to your own heart; consider, your unwillingness to return, is but a willingness to perish.

XII.   The *Pouring out* of the Heart.

Why dost thou conceal thy vows and thy wounds in thy closed breast? Let thy heart be spread out before God, as waters which are poured forth.

XIII.   The *Circumcision* of the Heart.

The cross supplies the handle; the spear, the edge; and the nails, the iron; that compose this knife: with it circumcise thy heart, and consecrate it to God.

XIV.   The *Contrition* of the Heart.

Into many thousand pieces would I break this heart, which hath wilfully rebelled against its Creator.

XV.   The *Humiliation* of the Heart.

Alas! the heart, delighting itself in lofty things, exalts itself too much, unless a weight be placed upon it, to keep it down.

XVI.   The *Softening* of the Heart.

My Heart, which is like icy marble, will melt like wax, when the fire of thy love (O God) begins to burn.

Translations of the Motto's in the SCHOOL.

ODE
XVII.   The *Cleansing* of the Heart.

A fountain flows from the wound in thy Husband's pierced side: in this, O spouse, wash away the defilements of thy heart.

XVIII.   The *Mirror* of the Heart.

For a discovery of the heart, sweet Jesus, look upon my heart; and let this sight imprint living wounds on thine.

XIX.   The *Sacrifice* of the Heart.

The sacrifice of a slain calf or bullock does not please God; that love, which gave me a heart, requires this heart for himself.

XX.   The *Weighing* of the Heart.

What thou gavest me as a great gift, is not so, unless an equal balance proves it to be of a proper weight.

XXI.   The *Defence* of the Heart.

Oh my Light! defend my heart with the shield of thy great sufferings, which your love for our hearts constrained you to bear.

XXII.   The *Trying* of the Heart.

I alone can search the immense abyss of the heart, which the mariner's plumb-line is unable to fathom.

XXII.   The *Levelling* of the Heart.

If you would have your heart upright, my daughter, bring it frequently for trial to the true level of mine.

XXV. The

Translations of the Motto's in the SCHOOL.

ODE XXIV.   The *Renewing* of the Heart.

Since all new things please, lay down thy old heart, O spouse, and take the new one which I place in its stead.

XXV.   The *Enlightening* of the Heart.

O God, thou light of light, thou only light of a blind world, dispel, by thy light, the thick darkness that obscures my heart.

XXVI.   The *Law-Table* of the Heart.

I now write a new law on the smooth, soft table of thy heart; whereas the old one, which was wrote on hard tables of stone, is for me (i. e. to fulfill).

XXVII.   The *Tilling* of the Heart.

Come then, O spouse, let the plough of thy cross break up the field of my heart, that into it thou mayest scatter the seeds of thy word.

XXVIII.   The *Seeding* of the Heart.

O divine Husbandman, commit thou the seed to the earth, lest the field of our hearts prove unfruitful to thee.

XXIX.   The *Watering* of the Heart.

Closed towards the earth; open towards heaven; let thy dew descend; that so the soil of my heart may flourish, and produce a variety of flowers.

XXX.   The *Flowers* of the Heart.

These lilies, O Spouse, which sprang from the seed thou sowedst, I consecrate to thee; to which also I add the soil in which they grew.

XXXI. The

Translations of the Motto's in the School.

ODE
XXXI. The *Keeping* of the Heart.

How well does that watchman keep the inclosed garden of his heart, whom the fear of God arms with a glittering sword!

XXXII. The *Watching* of the Heart.

Whilst sleep possesses my limbs, my watchful heart searches after thee; nor can I bear to be without thee, by night or by day.

XXXIII. The *Wounding* of the Heart.

O my Light, pierce thro' this heart with a thousand of thy most potent shafts; for the wounds given by thy right hand are medicines.

XXXIV. The *Inhabiting* of the Heart.

O my Light! may thy Spirit dwell in the temple of mine heart, that, loving thee with thine own love, O Spouse, thou may'st return it again to me.

XXXV. The *Enlarging* of the Heart.

How pleasant a thing it is to love that which heretofore the heart accounted bitter; even to run in a narrow way with an enlarged heart!

XXXVI. The *Inflaming* of the Heart.

Proceed, my Love, and inflame the inmost recesses of my heart, that, like a salamander, it may dwell in its native burning pile!

XXXVII. The *Ladder* of the Heart.

Would you, my beloved, ascend by a ladder to the heavenly seats? here first construct the steps in your own heart.

XXXVIII. The

Translations of the Motto's in the School.

Ode
XXXVIII.   The *Flying* of the Heart.

Who will give me the two wings of a dove, by which my heart, which is tired of the earth, may fly to heaven?

XXXIX.   The *Union* of the Heart.

Live, ye united minds and agreeing hearts, to whom one love gives but one will.

XL.   The *Rest* of the Heart.

My restless heart cannot dwell at ease in any (earthly) situation; for God alone is its centre, and only resting-place.

XLI. The *Bathing* of the Heart with the bloody Sweat.

The bath, which was filled with the bloody sweat of thy bleeding Spouse: come hither, sick heart, here is for you, what was appointed in Paradise.

"This is very obscure; but his meaning seems to
"be, that as it was apparently appointed in Pa-
"radise for man to live by the sweat of his brow,
"so by this bloody sweat the soul shall live."

XLII.   The *Binding* of the Heart with the Cords of Christ ('s Love).

My crimes, I confess, have bound thee with a cruel cord: may that sweeter cord of love bind my heart to thee.

XLIII.   Christ's Pillar, the *Prop* of the Heart.

My weak heart requires nor flowers nor apples to support it: this pillar of thine, O my Christ, is support enough.

Tranflations of the Motto's in the School.

ODE

XLIV. The Heart is the *Cup* to a thirfting Chrift.

Refufe the cup of gall, which the Jewifh people offered: but drink, O Spoufe, the new wine of a wounded heart.

XLV. The *Hedging* of the Heart with a Crown of Thorns.

That your thorns may not want rofes, let your Heart furnifh itfelf with that colour: this thorny diadem will keep all infernal wild beafts out of the garden.

XLVI. The Heart *pierced* with the Nails of God's fear.

Pierce through this heart of mine, with the nail of holy fear, O thou who waft nailed to the Crofs for me.

XLVII. The *New Wine* of the Heart cut of the Prefs of the Crofs.

Behold the Cyprian clufter of grapes is preft; accept, O heart, the rich-flavoured wine which flows from the wine-prefs of the crofs.

CPSIA information can be obtained
at www.ICGtesting.com
Printed in the USA
BVHW070716020321
601387BV00003B/98